CONDUCTING CASE STUDY RESEARCH

for BUSINESS *and* MANAGEMENT STUDENTS

CONDUCTING CASE STUDY RESEARCH

 for BUSINESS *and* MANAGEMENT STUDENTS

BILL LEE &
MARK N.K. SAUNDERS

Los Angeles | London | New Delhi
Singapore | Washington DC | Melbourne

Los Angeles | London | New Delhi
Singapore | Washington DC | Melbourne

SAGE Publications Ltd
1 Oliver's Yard
55 City Road
London EC1Y 1SP

SAGE Publications Inc.
2455 Teller Road
Thousand Oaks, California 91320

SAGE Publications India Pvt Ltd
B 1/I 1 Mohan Cooperative Industrial Area
Mathura Road
New Delhi 110 044

SAGE Publications Asia-Pacific Pte Ltd
3 Church Street
#10-04 Samsung Hub
Singapore 049483

Editor: Kirsty Smy
Assistant editor: Lyndsay Aitken
Production editor: Sarah Cooke
Marketing manager: Alison Borg
Cover design: Francis Kenney
Typeset by: C&M Digitals (P) Ltd, Chennai, India
Printed in the UK

Library of Congress Control Number: 2016959993

British Library Cataloguing in Publication data

A catalogue record for this book is available from
the British Library

ISBN 978-1-44627-416-3
ISBN 978-1-44627-417-0 (pbk)

At SAGE we take sustainability seriously. Most of our products are printed in the UK using FSC papers and boards.
When we print overseas we ensure sustainable papers are used as measured by the PREPS grading system.
We undertake an annual audit to monitor our sustainability.

CONTENTS

ABOUT THE AUTHORS

Bill Lee, PhD is Professor of Accounting at Sheffield University Management School where he has just completed his term as Head of the Accounting and Financial Management Division. He has a long-term interest in research methods and has been active in establishing communities of scholars interested in research methods. He was the inaugural secretary of the Research Methodology Special Interest Group of the British Academy of Management and the inaugural chair of the Research Methods and Research Practice Strategic Interest group of the European Academy of Management. In those capacities, he has organized numerous seminars, workshops, conference tracks and conferences. This part of his work has been supported by grants from a number of bodies including the Economic and Social Research Council, the Higher Education Academy and the Institute of Chartered Accountants in England and Wales. In addition to co-authoring *Conducting Case Study Research for Business and Management Students* with Mark, he has co-edited two important collections on research: *The Real Life Guide to Accounting Research* with Christopher Humphrey and *Challenges and Controversies in Management Research* with Catherine Cassell.

Mark N.K. Saunders, BA MSc PGCE PhD FCIPD is Professor of Business Research Methods at the Birmingham Business School and Director of Postgraduate Research Methods Training for the College of Social Sciences, University of Birmingham. He has a longstanding interest in researcher development having organized numerous colloquia and research methods summer schools. He is series editor of Edward Elgar's Handbooks of Research Methods in Management. In addition to co-authoring *Conducting Case Study Research for Business and Management Students* with Bill, he has co-authored and co-edited a range of other books on research methods including *Research Methods for Business Students* (currently in its 7th edition), *Doing Research in Business and Management*, the *Handbook of Research Methods on Trust* (currently in its 2nd edition) and the *Handbook of Research Methods on Human Resource Development*.

ABOUT THE SERIES EDITORS

Bill Lee, PhD is Professor of Accounting and Head of the Accounting and Financial Management Division at the University of Sheffield, UK. He has a long-standing interest in research methods and practice, in addition to his research into accounting and accountability issues. Bill's research has been published widely, including in: *Accounting Forum*; *British Accounting Review*; *Critical Perspectives on Accounting*; *Management Accounting Research*; *Omega*; and *Work, Employment & Society*. His publications in the area of research methods and practice include the co-edited collections *The Real Life Guide to Accounting Research* and *Challenges and Controversies in Management Research*.

Mark N.K. Saunders, BA MSc PGCE PhD FCIPD is Professor of Business Research Methods at Birmingham Business School, University of Birmingham, UK. His research interests are research methods, in particular methods for understanding intra organizational relationships; human resource aspects of the management of change, in particular trust within and between organizations; and small and medium-sized enterprises. Mark's research has been published in journals including *Journal of Small Business Management*, *Field Methods*, *Human Relations*, *Management Learning* and *Social Science and Medicine*. He has co-authored and co-edited a range of books including *Research Methods for Business Students* (currently in its 7th edition) and the *Handbook of Research Methods on Trust* (currently in its 2nd edition).

Vadake K. Narayanan is the Associate Dean for Research, Director of the Center for Research Excellence, and the Deloitte Touché Stubbs Professor of Strategy and Entrepreneurship in Drexel University, Philadelphia, PA. His articles have appeared in leading professional journals such as *Academy of Management Journal*, *Academy of Management Review*, *Accounting Organizations and Society*, *Journal of Applied Psychology*, *Journal of Management*, *Journal of Management Studies*, *Management*

Information Systems Quarterly, *R&D Management* and *Strategic Management Journal*. Narayanan holds a Bachelor's degree in Mechanical Engineering from the Indian Institute of Technology, Madras, a Postgraduate degree in Business Administration from the Indian Institute of Management, Ahmedabad, and a PhD in Business from the Graduate School of Business at the University of Pittsburgh, Pennsylvania.

EDITORS' INTRODUCTION TO THE *MASTERING BUSINESS RESEARCH METHODS* SERIES

Welcome to the *Mastering Business Research Methods* series. In recent years, there has been a great increase in the numbers of students reading Masters-level degrees across the business and management disciplines. A great number of these students have to prepare a dissertation towards the end of their degree programme in a time frame of three to four months. For many students, this takes place after their taught modules have finished and is expected to be an independent piece of work. Whilst each student is supported in their dissertation or research project by an academic supervisor, the student will need to find out more detailed information about the method that he or she intends to use. Before starting their dissertations or research projects these students have usually been provided with little more than an overview across a wide range of methods as preparation for this often daunting task. If you are one such student, you are not alone. As university professors with a deep interest in research methods, we have provided this series of books to help students like you. Each book provides detailed information about a particular method to support you in your dissertation. We understand both what is involved in Masters-level dissertations, and what help students need with regard to methods in order to excel when writing a dissertation. This series is the only one that is designed with the specific objective of helping Masters-level students to undertake and prepare their dissertations.

Each book in our series is designed to provide sufficient knowledge about either a method of data collection or a method of data analysis, and each book is intended to be read by the student when undertaking particular stages of the research process, such as data collection or analysis. Each book is written in a clear way by highly respected authors who have considerable experience of teaching and writing about research methods. To help students find their way around each book, we have utilized a standard format, with each book having been organized into six chapters:

- **Chapter 1** introduces the method, considers how the method emerged for what purposes, and provides an outline of the remainder of the book.
- **Chapter 2** addresses the underlying philosophical assumptions that inform the uses of particular methods.
- **Chapter 3** discusses the components of the relevant method.
- **Chapter 4** considers the way in which the different components may be organized to use the method.
- **Chapter 5** provides examples of published studies that have used the method.
- **Chapter 6** concludes by reflecting on the strengths and weaknesses of that method.

We hope that reading your chosen books helps you in your dissertation.

Bill Lee, Mark N.K. Saunders and Vadake K. Narayanan

1

INTRODUCTION TO CASE STUDIES

INTRODUCTION

The purpose of this book is to provide a guide to students who decide to incorporate one or more case studies into the data collection processes that they conduct in preparation of a Masters-level dissertation. We will elaborate on what case studies are below, but a provisional definition is that a case study entails a decision to study an instance, institution or phenomenon primarily as interesting *per se*, rather than as a representative of a broader population. This initial decision will subsequently involve the researcher in fieldwork, collecting evidence about the phenomenon from a range of sources to seek to develop a multidimensional understanding of the case.

Masters-level students are our primary audience but this book may also provide a primer for students studying for research degrees such as PhDs or for others who are considering using case studies for the first time. In offering some form of guide, we outline two broad approaches to help structure the discussion. In defining them as broad approaches, we are intending that the reader recognizes that we are presenting each as a genre that may embrace a number of different variants, rather than a definite prescription of a single best way of conducting each type of case study. One broad approach may be considered as orthodox and starts with the reading of literature and progresses in a linear way through the development of a research question or questions, design of research, collection of data, analysis of data and writing up of the research. The other recognizes greater iteration and will be referred to throughout as an emergent approach. As will become clear below, we do not intend the term emergent to imply that it is an approach that is only just being developed; instead we use the term to infer that the case will be developed as the research proceeds when the researcher encounters new circumstances and ideas, often in unanticipated ways. So the emergent approach will not necessarily start from the reading of the literature, but may instead start with a problem or an observation or some data in the form of anecdotal evidence that the researcher finds interesting and then progresses from there to include the stages that appear in the orthodox approach, although often not in the same order as takes place in the orthodox approach.

The two approaches are not necessarily dichotomous. Indeed, some readers who are experienced in the conduct of case studies and conversant with a broad range of literature on case studies and research methods more generally may suggest that this book simplifies what some writers on orthodox case studies advocate, or it combines elements of a range of different approaches into emergent cases, or it does not centralize alternative ways of dividing case studies such as by the epistemological preferences of the researcher as is used by some other writers (e.g., Boblin et al., 2013). We recognize some legitimacy in such criticisms.

We do, however, have two main reasons for organizing the book according to the chronological order in which stages in the research process are carried out. The first main reason is that the two approaches reflect two broad traditions that are presented below when we discuss the history of case studies. The first approach is based on the principles of experimental psychology where research questions are defined within tightly defined boundaries and there are then attempts to control the boundaries and collect evidence within those boundaries so that the original research questions and findings addressed to those questions are seen to have validity. The second approach is that of ethnographic research stemming originally from anthropological studies where boundaries are not known, and where issues of interest deemed most worthy of expression in written-up findings only emerge as the research progresses. The former lends itself to a linear progression through the stages of research. The latter can accommodate a much less rigid advance through the different stages in the research process. As you may be undertaking your first research project, you may have had limited opportunities to familiarize yourself with different traditions, so this book provides you with these alternatives.

The second main reason to justify our organization of the book according to differences in the chronological order in the stages that the case study is conducted, is that the two approaches tend to reflect what happens in practice when experienced academics undertake case studies. Cases do start at different stages, not least because people may have made a number of observations, or had a number of experiences over time and they may have started to formulate ideas of why those events had occurred. In effect, they had started to define a problem before they had conducted an extensive review of the literature. Alternatively, a problem may be suggested to a researcher by someone who then provides access to evidence (see, for example, Buchanan, 2012). Only some case studies will start because people identify a gap in the literature and progress from there to conduct of the case. If the research of experienced academics progresses in different ways, it would be inappropriate to suggest that people with less experience should not also have a choice of alternatives, especially when many Masters-level students are mature and have numerous experiences that might help in defining a research problem. This book is written in a way where it will not only provide a guide to using case studies in research that has different starting points but the information provided will also help you to document a systematic explanation of what you have done and why you did it. It is worth noting at this stage that some other authors also write about 'teaching cases' that document a scenario and ask students to consider issues surrounding the scenario from different vantage points. We deliberately avoid consideration of teaching cases as the purpose of this book is to provide guidance around using case studies in research.

The objectives of the remainder of this chapter are threefold. The first is to expand on ideas of what constitutes case studies and the two alternative approaches. These are described here as either orthodox that involves the advanced definition of the protocol of the specific case study as a comprehensive research strategy, or emergent where the case study is perceived as a strategic choice that presupposes only using one or more institutions or instances as cases, but the exact way in which knowledge about those cases will be derived and used to add to our understanding is not pre-defined and will be finalized as a research strategy as the research progresses. The second objective is to discuss the origins of case studies partly as a means to providing an understanding of why they have been developed as ways of conducting research and to help illuminate the differences in the two approaches that are outlined. The final objective of this chapter is to outline the remainder of the book.

WHAT IS A CASE STUDY?

One of the things that may surprise – and confuse – a reader new to research when reviewing the literature on case studies is the different terms that are used to explain what case studies are. For example, Janckowicz (2005: 220) has described case studies as a research method which may be defined as 'a systematic and orderly approach taken to the collection and analysis of data'. For Janckowicz (2005: 221) case studies will then embrace different techniques – which are identical to what others have described as 'methods'– that comprise 'particular step-by-step procedures which you can follow in order to gather data and analyse them for the information they contain'. Robert Yin (2014), who is probably the best-known author on case studies, sometimes uses the term 'method' to describe a case study and at other times suggests that a case study is a research strategy which will contain a number of methods. This definition of case studies as a research strategy embracing a number of methods is one echoed by a number of other writers (see, for example, Hartley, 2004).

The above definitions are all aligned with orthodox approaches that tend to suggest that all research components that lead to a research output known as a case study may be collapsed into a set of decisions in advance of the study taking place.

For this reason, this book will view such approaches as seeing case studies as a research strategy. That strategy will progress through a route that is primarily linear as presented in Figure 1.1.

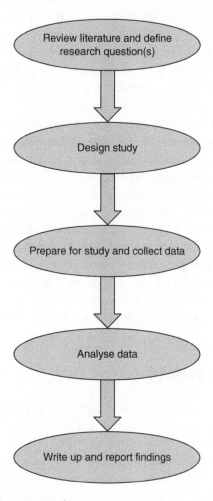

Figure 1.1   Orthodox linear approach

It starts with a thorough literature review that will result in the formulation of clear theoretical propositions often expressed as research questions. The research then progresses to a plan for the conduct of the research which will entail theorizing about the cases in ways that will allow the generation of answers to the research questions, the evidence that will be necessary and the people whose position will enable provision of that evidence and then to the execution of that plan. Although some authors may acknowledge that some stages may be repeated, we have focussed on the aspects of linearity when providing an outline of the orthodox approach in Figure 1.1 to help distinguish the difference between orthodox and emergent approaches. The advanced definition of what is to be done in the course of such an orthodox case study is usually expressed in the form of a research protocol – see Chapter 4 for more on this. Unplanned divergence from that protocol is a violation of the research and is likely to create bias. The orthodox approach relies heavily on propositional knowledge – i.e., that which has been expressed in formulated and shared statements – derived from the literature review and determines the scope of the research. The advantage of this approach is that if the research has been designed properly to make a contribution to the literature – and perhaps to resolve a problem within a case study organization – and the case can be executed as initially conceived, early stages of the research process may be written up as the case is progressing (see Yin, 2014: 195) and the dissertation project should be completed and written up in a timely way with the desired outcome. This type of approach clearly has its supporters (e.g., Crowe et al., 2011; Yin, 2014) and it may be one which you seek to – and your dissertation supervisor encourages you to – utilize. In subsequent chapters, this book will outline how to conduct orthodox case studies.

There are, however, drawbacks with orthodox case studies. Firstly, propositional knowledge may not have captured experiential, empathetic and tacit knowledge, which can enhance understanding. To focus only on propositional knowledge is to risk excluding these other forms of knowledge from the case study. Everyone exists in a range of different communities and will be affected by a wide range of different issues. It seems less than sensible to suggest that they should not seek to think analytically about – and document – what they know about those communities and issues simply because they have not yet conducted an extensive literature view. Secondly, a reluctance to wait until a literature review has been conducted could lead to the forfeit of opportunities that provide 'accidental access' to an organization that constitutes an interesting site to study a particular problem (Otley and Berry, 1994: 51). Conversely, the ideal site to examine a particular research question that follows from a literature review may not be identifiable or accessible. Thirdly, once the case is started, there is a danger that the specified case study protocol could become a straightjacket that precludes new opportunities to gather evidence as they arise, or the case could lead to many false starts as new projects have to be started if new, important insights become available. Encouragement to miss such opportunities is perhaps most evident in Yin's (2014: 55) discussion of holistic cases when he says:

> The initial study questions may have reflected one orientation, but as the case study proceeds, a different orientation may emerge, and the evidence begins to address different research questions. ... you need to avoid such unsuspected slippage; if the relevant research questions really do change, you should simply start over again, with a new research design.

The alternative approach to case studies being proposed here recognizes both the other forms of knowledge that enhance understanding that may need to be embodied in a case study at some point and that qualitative research that involves naturalistic settings tends 'to be much more fluid and flexible than quantitative research in that it emphasizes discovering novel or unanticipated findings and the possibility of altering research plans in research to such serendipitous occurrences' (Patton, 2015: 240). Not surprisingly, Stake (1995: 28) has said:

> Researchers differ on how much they want to have their research questions identified in advance. Case study fieldwork regularly takes the research in unexpected directions, so too much commitment in advance is problematic.

In suggesting an alternative of emergent case studies, the objective is to realize the benefits of alternative forms of knowledge identified above and to exercise the degree of flexibility to respond to events that were not anticipated, but which might enhance the understanding that can be derived from a case. For these reasons, the suggestion here is that an emergent approach will simply view a case study as a strategic choice. The nature of the choice that is made is that empirical study of one or more institutions or instances of a phenomenon is the best way of answering a particular research question. How the choice of cases is made, decisions on the defining aspects of the cases, the theorization of any relationship between the case and a wider population, the interesting aspects of the case requiring focus and the ways to derive data to address the interesting aspects of the case are all other decisions that will be made in the course of the research. As such the strategic choice of using one or more cases may be built into a range of different research strategies that will involve conducting case studies and employing them in a dissertation, but which will emerge as the research progresses.

Figure 1.2 adapts what is presented in Figure 1.1 to show the general course of development in emergent approaches to case studies. In the diagram, the definition of the research question(s) is decoupled from the conduct of the literature review. The research questions are not seen as unimportant - indeed, they remain central to the construction of the case and are likely to guide many actions; however, there is acknowledgement of the possibility that 'the best research questions evolve during the study' (Stake, 1995: 33). Thus, in the diagram, the definition of the research question(s) could take place at a range of stages, both before or after each of the respective stages of reviewing the literature, designing the study, collecting the data, preparing for further study and collecting more data or analysing data. It will all depend on what knowledge - either formal propositional or experiential, empathetic and tacit - you have already acquired and the extent to which you have identified a phenomenon as a problem. As the diagram illustrates, there may be considerable movement backwards and forwards between different stages and some might overlap. For example, the identification of an initial problem could lead to a provisional design of a study and even the collection of some data to check that the problem may be significant simultaneous to an initial literature review, leading to a refined definition of the research questions.

Figure 1.2 Emergent approach

It is, however, important to emphasize two points with regards to the different approaches. Firstly, neither Figure 1.1 nor Figure 1.2 has a stage of ethical approval. A requirement to obtain ethical approval before conducting research that involves the collection of data from human participants is increasingly common and some universities will not allow you to use data that has been collected without ethical approval. It is, thus, important that you check your own institution's ethical procedures and comply with them when following either of the journeys represented in Figure 1.1 or Figure 1.2. Secondly, the final writing-up and reporting of findings to the appropriate audiences is accepted here as the last stage for a Masters-level student when preparing a dissertation, although it may be that the work involved in the dissertation will be continued in some form or other afterwards.

In identifying orthodox and emergent approaches to case studies, the intention here is not to suggest that the outcome will necessarily be any different. As Yin (2014: 16; see also Tsang, 2014: 370) reports the product of a case study is 'an empirical inquiry that investigates a contemporary phenomenon (the "case") in depth and within its real-world context, especially when the boundaries between phenomenon and context may not be clearly evident'. Similarly, orthodox and emergent approaches will each recognize other aspects of Yin's (2014: 16) definition of a distinctive and complex situation being studied that will require multiple sources of data and will involve some development of theory, although – as previously indicated – not necessarily in the same order or for the same objective or to address the same research questions. The nature of the case, if an institution, may be either generic such as industry, sector, specific country or population, or it may be more specific such as a particular corporation, responsibility or programme of tasks. The nature of the case, if a phenomenon, may be an event, a co-existing series of events or a ritual. The understanding proposed may be a general one to be represented as shared, or it may be from a particular viewpoint such as line managers' view of, or influence on, personnel practices at their organization. The aim will be to provide rich descriptions of both the phenomenon and the context for the purpose of providing new knowledge about the case and/or theoretical constructs.

As the objective of a Masters dissertation is to report clearly to an academic audience – and sometimes to a practitioner one as well – it is just as important when pursuing an emergent approach as it is with an orthodox approach to keep systematic records of the evidence that has been collected – even though the way of conducting the research was not defined fully at the outset – and link that evidence to propositional statements found in published academic work. Similarly, it is just as important when utilizing an orthodox approach as it is with an emergent approach to seek to capture and convey much of the implicit, unstated understandings that are commonly known by the participants, in order to be able to provide understanding and a convincing account of what is happening in the case. In linking your findings to the different forms of knowledge that you have utilized, it is important to describe the ideas with which you started your research and how these developed in the course of your project so as to convey an accurate account of the conduct of your study. As Otley and Berry (1994: 47) point out, a common failing in case study research is that it is often not clear whether the ideas that are reported are the ones that the researcher started with at the outset or whether they are ones that have been adopted in the course of the research.

Table 1.1 summarizes the differences that we have identified between orthodox and emergent approaches to case studies in this section. It will be useful to review

Table 1.1 Key distinctions between orthodox and emergent case study approaches

	Orthodox	Emergent
Initial type of primary knowledge	Propositional from formal theories that are brought in from the outside	Possibly partly propositional but also derived from within the case and often experiential, empathetic and tacit
Point of conduct of principal literature review	Outset	Throughout
Point of definition of principal research questions	Immediately after principal literature review	Any time before completion of fieldwork
Nature of choice	Integrated strategy with clear protocol	Series of strategic choices that are fluid and emergent throughout the case
Process of case	Primarily linear	Primarily iterative

this table to make sure that you understand these differences before proceeding further. If you already have a research question to study in mind, you might also think briefly at this point about the issues in the left-hand column and whether you are already leaning towards either an orthodox or an emergent approach and how you are intending to proceed through the stages outlined in either Figure 1.1 or Figure 1.2.

WHY USE A CASE STUDY?

One of the distinctions that will be evident in the next chapter is that of particularization versus generalization. One of the claims for quantitative survey research is its utility if you seek to make statistical generalizations about a population. By contrast, case studies are often criticized for not allowing generalization. While such a view of case studies has been challenged (see, for example, Tsang, 2014) – and in Chapter 2 we will return to consider how you might use case studies in a research strategy where you wish to generalize your findings – it is important to emphasize that a key strength of case studies is that of particularization. This refers to the capability to study the particular institution or phenomenon in depth to identify its unique characteristics and the ways in which those unique characteristics combine in a very specific way to produce a particular outcome and to provide an explanation based on those unique characteristics and combinations. A case may be interesting in its own right and does not require wider inferences to give it greater value. It is this strength that has been a feature of case studies when one looks at their historic development.

In the social sciences, case studies originated in early twentieth century anthropology as authors such as E.E. Evans-Pritchard conducted systematic ethnographic studies of other cultures using participant-observation methods with long periods of fieldwork in a different society. Case studies were then transferred through the adoption of ethnographic approaches in sociology as sociologists researched parts of their own indigenous culture; one of the most famous being the Chicago School's urban studies. Although there had been piecemeal uses of cases in the general area of management previously, such as Taylor's (1911) use of Schmidt at Bethlehem Steel Company to illustrate the principles of Scientific Management, this latter period saw a number of ethnographic studies of workplaces. This latter tranche of studies included the work of Donald Roy (1959) and Michael Burawoy (1979) in the USA and Tom Lupton (1963) and Huw Beynon (1973) in the UK. These studies provided a crossover between the disciplines of sociology and the more emergent disciplines related to management. Indeed, Tom Lupton was one of the academics recruited to the area of management as Schools of Business or Management were established in the UK as part of the expansion of higher education in the 1960s. Knowledge of methods was, thus, transferred by the movement of academics between disciplines in the UK.

A common feature of the work of all the above authors is that, regardless of their disciplinary and geographical context, they all provided rich insights into areas of social life that were not previously understood. As the academics immersed themselves in the everyday life of people that they studied, the ideas or theories they developed tended to emerge from the empirical evidence that they collected.

In some quarters, however, their approach was considered as not scientific, lacking in the methodological rigour that would enable their findings to be made generalizable. Perhaps a little unfortunately, one response to this criticism helped to establish a new orthodoxy in the disciplines that make up business and management. Robert Yin – who is an experimental psychologist (Campbell, 1984) – produced a work that married a positivist epistemology to an experimental design to propose highly defined ways of using case studies. A reading of Yin's book, first published in 1984 and now in its fifth edition, gives insight into how he seeks to transfer some of the logic of control from experiments into the design of case studies. Yin's book became popular in the subsidiary disciplines of the Business and Management field. Lee (1999: 15) reports that Yin's book was one of the three top methodological works for citations across four important American journals; namely, *Academy of Management Journal*, *Administrative Science Quarterly*, *Organizational Science* and *Strategic Management Journal*. Yin's book offered an alternative to the statistical generalization found in quantitative survey research, to allow a small number of case studies to be seen as having wider applicability. The alternative he proposed was that of theoretical or analytic generalization based on the generalizability of theoretical propositions to different situations. Yin's approach has shaped the orthodoxy in the Business and Management field. For example, Tsang (2014) conducted a review of the 25 articles based on case studies that appeared in the American *Academy of Management Journal* between 2008 and 2012 and found that all sought to use theoretical generalization.

Since that time, others have challenged some of the ideas evident in Yin's orthodox approach and highlighted the potential of case studies to utilize experiential and empathetic knowledge, retain flexibility in the course of fieldwork and produce understanding of a unique institution or phenomenon through particularization (Stake, 1995: 7; Lee et al., 2007). Proposals on how to utilize orthodox case studies will be outlined in the next chapter, along with suggestions of how to conduct the alternative of emergent case studies that are identified above. What is meant by an emergent approach is not incompatible with the ethnographic case studies identified above where, instead of there being a tendency to pre-design all aspects of the research, there is acknowledgement that some decisions about the research will be made as the case progresses. Thus, in your research, you may choose to use a case study because you aspire to understand whether your findings may be generalized to other units of analysis, or because you wish to understand the unique qualities of the case as a single unit of analysis.

OUTLINE OF REMAINDER OF BOOK

So far, we have outlined two approaches to undertaking case studies. The remainder of the book is organized in the following way. In Chapter 2, we discuss issues that should be considered when conducting a case study using either an emergent or orthodox approach. These issues, which will never be far from the surface until the research is completed, include:

- The philosophical position of the researcher;
- The impact of the philosophical position on the design of the research;
- The ways in which the philosophical position and the design will affect the relationship between the cases that are studied and any wider population of cases which will affect the capacity to theorize from the research;
- The types of logic that may be employed when theorizing;
- The different strategies for selecting cases; and
- The factors that will affect the choice of data collection methods to be used in a case.

This leads into Chapter 3 that provides a discussion of the tasks that have to be completed in the course of a case study. Chapter 4 then brings together the contents of the preceding chapters to discuss just how both orthodox and emergent case studies might be conducted. Chapter 5 provides examples of published cases where different approaches have been adopted. Chapter 6 concludes by reflecting on the strengths and limitations of case studies. A glossary of key terms is also provided at the end of the book.

SUMMARY

This chapter has distinguished between two approaches to case studies - the orthodox that sees the case study as an integrated, pre-defined, research strategy so that research proceeds in a linear way, and the emergent that sees the case study as a strategic choice that is made and there are movements backwards and forwards between different stages in the research process in the course of the research as other decisions of how to conduct the case study and for what purpose are built into the research strategy as the research proceeds. Why orthodox cases gained prominence in management disciplines has been discussed, although the understanding brought by each type of case has also been outlined, as has the remainder of the book. Before you proceed to the next chapter, you may wish to think about the exercise that is shown in Box 1.1 on the following page that illustrates the differences between orthodox and emergent case studies that have been made in this chapter and which will be evident in subsequent chapters.

Box 1.1   Questions for reflection

First:

- Write down a research question based on the literature that you know from any of the modules that you have studied.
- Identify a case to be studied that will allow you to address that question.
- Think about the type of evidence that you will need from that case to answer the research question that you have posed.

Then:

- Think of an institution or phenomenon that you know well.
- Think about something in that institution or phenomenon that you do not necessarily understand in some way.
- Think about how you could use your knowledge and understanding of an institution or phenomenon that you know well to formulate a research question to investigate the part that you do not know well.

2

UNDERSTANDING CASE STUDIES

INTRODUCTION

This chapter provides an understanding of the ways in which case studies contribute to knowledge. The discussion will build on the distinction between orthodox and emergent approaches to case studies made in the previous chapter. In that context, the issues below may be seen either as aspects of a case study research strategy in orthodox approaches, or as additional strategic choices that will be made while conducting a case study in an emergent approach. It should be emphasized that the purpose for making the distinction between orthodox and emergent approaches is to highlight that there are different ways to conduct case studies and both have been – and may be – used in a wide variety of successful research projects. It is important to utilize the best resources that are available to answer the chosen research questions given the starting position of the researcher.

As this chapter is about how case studies may be used to contribute to knowledge, it is helpful at this point to identify at which stages the theory that will make the contribution to knowledge will be developed by reference to Figure 1.1 and 1.2. In the orthodox approach, the initial statement of the theories that are being examined will be developed at the time of the literature review. This will help to define the types of questions that are asked, of whom, from what populations and under which conditions the theory being examined may or may not apply. Once the data are collected, they will be analysed and the extent to which the theory has been confirmed or refined will be established so that the findings and the theoretical contribution to knowledge can be written up. By contrast, in an emergent approach, while the start of the development of the theoretical contribution may commence from the beginning of the study, the idea may simply be at the level of being experiential or empathetic and at least partially tacit as the researcher is aware of a problem, but he or she does not know – and is not yet able to articulate – its exact nature to allow a theoretical contribution to be made. Some empirical research may need to be conducted before the tacit understandings of the relationship are made explicit and research questions are formulated. It is only after the research questions have been fully defined, however, that the nature of the theoretical contribution will start to take shape. It is also likely that further new ideas will appear in the course of fieldwork and so theory will be extended at that point and systematized as the analysis of the data proceeds.

The rest of the chapter seeks to elaborate on the basis of knowledge generated by case studies and will progress in the following way. The first section provides a general classification of philosophical approaches as a means of elaborating on the different assumptions about the nature of knowledge and the world that is studied in orthodox and emergent approaches to case studies. The following section considers the implications of the underlying philosophy for the development of concepts and their linkages to the case through different types of logic to provide additions to knowledge. The next section will reflect on the type of contribution that your research may make by elaborating on the concepts of particularization and generalization. We then consider how to select appropriate cases to ensure the objectives of your contribution are met. The final substantive section considers the ways in which research involving case studies may be evaluated according to your specific philosophical predilections and choices.

DEFINING THE CASE: SAYING WHAT IT IS POSSIBLE TO STUDY AND WHAT THE CASE CONVEYS

In seeking to understand the nature of the knowledge that you may obtain from a case study, it is important to define your ontological and epistemological positions. Ontology refers to your understanding of the nature of reality. Epistemology refers to your view of what constitutes valid and legitimate knowledge. It is possible to classify different epistemological and ontological positions along a two axes schema with the ontological positions shown on the vertical axis and the epistemological positions shown on the horizontal axis, as represented in Table 2.1.

Table 2.1 Relationship between epistemological and ontological positions and approaches to case studies

Epistemology ⇒ Ontology ⬇	Positivist	Interpretivist
Realist	Orthodox most likely	Both orthodox and emergent studies possible
Constructivist	Not possible	Emergent more possible

The epistemological and ontological positions shown in the table will be explained briefly. A positivist epistemological perception that a phenomenon is external and independent of the researcher allows that phenomenon to be known objectively by utilizing scientific methods, while an interpretivist epistemology recognizes that there may be different interpretations of the same event. At an ontological level, realists view external phenomena to be independent of their participation. In contrast, constructivists view reality as constructed through social interactions between those participating. The quarter of Table 2.1 that represents the intersection between positivist epistemology and constructivist ontology may be discounted as it is not possible to reconcile the external independent existence of phenomena with a reality that has been constructed socially in interactions. In seeking to build on the distinctions that were made in Chapter 1 between an orthodox and an emergent approach, it is useful to state that the combination of viewing reality as independent and external and researchers as able to be objective in conducting research encourages a tendency towards orthodox case study approaches as indicated by the upper left-hand quarter in Table 2.1. In contrast, a researcher's acceptance that research participants contribute to the construction of reality and there are different ways of interpreting that reality may lend itself to a more emergent case study approach as indicated in the bottom right-hand quarter of Table 2.1. It is possible to combine realist ontology with beliefs in external structures that may help to shape actions – in different situations – with an interpretivist epistemology that acknowledges that different participants can give different meanings to activities and structures that constrain them and to then take actions to change and modify the structures, producing a new reality over time. A predilection for realist ontology may allow a researcher to conduct an orthodox case while subscription to an interpretivist epistemology may lead the same researcher to undertake an emergent case. Both possibilities are presented in the upper right-hand quarter of Table 2.1.

If an orthodox case study approach is adopted, it is likely that it will proceed in the way outlined previously in Figure 1.1. It is, thus, necessary to conduct a literature review to identify a gap that may be addressed, at least partially, by conducting one or more case studies. The literature review will also include you familiarizing yourself with a number of different theories that can help to explain the phenomenon of interest. Once the research question has been articulated, it will be broken down into component propositions around which empirical evidence may be collected. Relevant cases – or units of analysis – will be identified according to some form of selection logic that will be discussed later in this chapter, and methods for collecting evidence that addresses the propositions will be selected and built into a research protocol. The research protocol will also include a detailed description of how the methods are to be used such as how the questions are to be asked in an interview – for discussion of methods, see Chapters 3 and 4. An example of such an approach is illustrated in Box 2.1.

Box 2.1   An example of an orthodox approach to designing case study research

Susan has decided to do her Masters dissertation on whether large companies in the energy-related industries adopt an effective 'green' human resource management (HRM) strategy by instituting practices that promote the saving and re-use of resources by their employees. Susan has previously read some literature on green HRM and she has found an academic study that indicates how many companies have introduced recycle bins, movement-sensitive lighting, etc. However, she theorizes that companies in the energy-related industries are less likely to engage in 'green', energy-saving practices because they profit most from maximum energy usage and she formulates the following proposition for investigation: 'Companies that supply energy as a core component of their business are less likely to pursue energy-saving initiatives through their employees than are companies that do not supply energy as a core component of their business.' As Susan has data about the latter from the existing literature, she intends to focus her case studies on companies in the energy sector.

She starts by ensuring the validity of her concepts of energy-saving – which she defines as a net reduction in the usage of finite resources by the organization through less energy-consuming methods, recycling, re-use and re-fashioning of resources – and HRM – which she defines as policies that are designed to promote employees of an organization pursuing specific goals, in this instance, energy-saving policies.

Susan decides to focus her attention on the gas industry and she compiles a list of gas suppliers from which she selects one large and one small corporation. Susan then identifies the sources of data which will enable her to answer her research questions. She decides that the data that she will need from her research to answer her question are: (i) Specific policy documents that each corporation has prepared around recycling and saving of energy; (ii) An interview with the Human Resource Director or Senior Human Resource Manager to identify the existence and objectives of any policies and practices to motivate their respective workforces to recycle materials, etc. and to save energy; and (iii) A tour of a site to look at the implementation of policies.

At this stage, she outlines her research protocol, prepares information sheets and consent forms for prospective participants and applies for ethical approval to conduct her research.

By contrast, the decision to use a case study with an emergent approach may arise from a range of considerations, many of which start off as unarticulated and are slowly drawn out to form a research question and knowledge of different literatures may come together in a way not anticipated at the outset as the researcher starts to articulate the idea and the sources of knowledge to which they have access. This approach might be used when a researcher combines an interpretivist epistemology with either a constructivist or realist ontology, but it may be more likely to emerge in situations where the researcher is already familiar with the ethnographic context of the research. For an example of such an approach, see Box 2.2 below. In other words, the case may be more likely to proceed in the way outlined previously in Figure 1.2.

Box 2.2   An example of an emergent approach to designing case study research

Pietar is an office manager at an office of a medium-sized firm of Chartered Accountants in Dresden. He has been given a sabbatical from his job to study for a Masters in Accounting and Finance. In his job, he has been impressed by the approach of the professional accountants in his practice, who talk about the exercise of their professional judgement to realize valued goals of stewardship and proper observation of the rules for economic activity. Such ideas resonate with his understanding of what constitutes a profession which he learned about during his time as a social science undergraduate when he encountered theories that suggested a profession was an institute whose members pursued higher values, or their members were people who exhibited qualities that could not be codified when making decisions.

In the course of his MSc in Accounting and Finance, Pietar has been introduced to a range of accounting scandals, such as Enron, where firms of accountants have been implicated for not operating with the highest moral standards when auditing organizations. He has also heard a number of his peers express a desire to become accountants because of the high salaries that some accountants earn, rather than because of higher moral values. Pietar starts to wonder whether the values that his peers are expressing are consistent with the values that prevail at a medium-sized firm of accountants like the one from which he has his sabbatical.

Pietar takes stock of what he knows already. He already has access to ethical statements from the accounting professional bodies and he has sometimes looked at them when changes to ethical standards and codes have been made to understand why the changes have been introduced. He has the accumulated knowledge of the values that have existed in the organization where he works and knowledge of the ways in which his firm induct trainee accountants. Similarly, he knows some aspects of the attitudes of his student peers that he has experienced

(Continued)

during his Masters programme up to that date. Pietar formulates a research question that asks whether the education of Masters-level students in accounting contain sufficient ethical content to prepare them for employment in medium-sized firms of accountants like his own.

He decides that he will conduct a case study of the ethical component in the education of Masters-level students at the university where he is studying and a case study of ethics at the firm from which he has a sabbatical to see the extent to which they correspond. He proposes to do the former by analysing the content of the syllabus for his course and conducting a group interview with some of his student peers and an interview with the director of the programme. He plans to do the latter by looking at the ethical statements from the accounting professional institutes of which accountants in his firm are members, documenting the induction process for new accountants at his firm and interviewing the partner responsible for overseeing training. He prepares a formal outline of his research protocol, his research instruments, information sheets for participants and consent forms and he applies for ethical approval. Having decided on his research question, he then conducts a literature review about ethical formation of accounting entrants through both the curriculum and through professional training to help him put his study into an intellectual context.

APPROACHES, CONCEPTS AND EXPLANATIONS

As with any approach to data collection, when researchers use a case study, they inevitably make assumptions about their capability to use concepts to represent the phenomenon that is to be studied and to generate explanations about how and why that phenomenon occurs. These assumptions will differ according to the type of epistemological and ontological ideas that tend to underlie orthodox and emergent case studies. While some orthodox approaches might acknowledge that it is not possible to separate out parts of a case study in practice, the parts are deemed analytically separable and so capable of being represented by different concepts. This analytical separation and attribution of separate concepts then permits explanations of causal links between them (see, for example, Yin, 2014: 20). Once the causal links have been identified in a case, replication of findings in different contexts will allow the construction of nomothetic knowledge – that is, generalizable statements.

In comparison, while some of the ontological and epistemological assumptions that permit the emergent approach acknowledge that it might be possible to suggest concepts to represent parts of the same phenomenon as different components, that is neither the same as those components being practically separable nor does it provide evidence of a causal relationship between the reputed separable components.

In effect, while those ideas may purport to represent an empirical reality, they may not do so. Perceptions of components as different and separable deny the extent to which they may be inextricably linked in a phenomenon in a specific naturalistic setting. It is the perceptions that order the understanding of the empirical reality rather than the empirical reality producing the perceptions. As any phenomenon or system is multidimensional, different participants will have different understandings of it, so it is important to acknowledge that there could be multiple understandings of the topic which makes it necessary to specify from which vantage point the reality of the phenomenon or system is to be understood. Furthermore, given the capability of human actors to choose a range of different options, it is not possible to talk in absolute causal terms and there is no reason to expect any phenomenon to appear in exactly the same format elsewhere. The key objective is, thus, to explain why the particular case appeared as it did; that is to generate an ideographic form of knowledge. This is not to deny the existence of concepts, but it is to state that for some authors the concepts are inseparable from the phenomena which they purport to represent and are themselves embedded in a wider cultural context and broader sets of meanings.

When considering the development of concepts to help explain a phenomenon, the level at which the concept or explanation will be developed, should be identified. In addressing this issue, it is of value to refer to Llewelyn's (2003; c.f. Yin, 2014: 41) helpful classification of five levels of understanding. The five levels are: metaphor; differentiation; conceptualization; context-bound explanation within settings; and context-free 'grand' explanations. A metaphor is a familiar form of experience or knowledge which may be used to make sense of something unfamiliar. For example, someone may feel a tension when encountering a new situation at work in a way that makes him or her apprehensive about addressing that situation or completing his or her work. By using the metaphor of tension, that person would have succeeded in bringing to the surface parts of his or her knowledge that when something is new in the workplace, he or she experienced a similar feeling of tension. In effect, the metaphor served as a tool through which the person's own tacit knowledge was articulated. In the same way, researchers may gain access to understanding research participants' tacit and experiential knowledge about a phenomenon that is being studied by asking those others whether they can liken what the researcher is studying to everyday things that the researcher may be familiar with. Differentiation involves marking off a metaphor from others, often through a pairing of two metaphors, comparing and contrasting them and stating the nature of their relationship to one another. So, to continue the example above, the person could use the metaphors of both tension and excitement to seek an understanding of what happens to him or her. For example, the person may know that he or she experiences excitement when he or she is about to play a competitive sports game. So, the person could compare the tension that he or she feels when confronted with new circumstances in the work situation and the excitement experienced when about to play a competitive sports game. The person might recognize similarities in the two metaphors by noting that while they each have a combination of something that is known of the workplace and the sports game, they also have something unfamiliar in terms of the new circumstance in the workplace and a different team against which the sports match is being played. The person might start to distinguish between the different experiences by noting that while one involves something which he or she is paid to do, the other involves an activity that is voluntary. Also, while the tension experienced at work is unpleasant, the excitement experienced in anticipation of playing sport is enjoyable.

The third level in Llewelyn's schema is that of conceptualization. This classification marks a shift away from external comparisons of qualities of a phenomenon with other things to start to articulate a phenomenon's intrinsic qualities by defining the different ways in which a concept is distinct. To continue with the example, the person may start to note that when the state of tension is experienced at work, he or she also experiences some physical changes such as his or her heart racing faster, his or her hands starting to sweat and the experience of finding it difficult to concentrate. The person might, thus, conceptualize that what he or she has experienced is workplace stress. The fourth level of context-bound explanations within settings link social, organizational or individual phenomena to their settings, thus, drawing a range of differentiations and concepts into a broader schema. In the example provided, the person may realize that the reason why he or she experienced workplace stress is because he or she is worried about failing in his or her paid employment and the reason for that fear is because the employer has not provided any training to help cope with this situation. The final level of grand explanations provides a meta-narrative that is applicable to a range of different institutions. In the example above, the person might theorize all the circumstances when somebody is likely to feel stress and the reasons for that. While all these different levels above may feature in your dissertation research if you choose to use case studies, it is most likely that you will focus on the third and fourth of the levels above, namely, an individual phenomenon which it is necessary to study in its context such as a particular type or cause of stress; or a type of institution in which particular types of phenomena of interest are manifest such as microenterprises.

At this stage, it is appropriate to introduce different types of logic that may be used to link ideas and explanations to empirical observations. To do this, it is first necessary to understand two types of knowledge. Etic knowledge is that which originates from outside. An example is theories that already exist in the literature prior to the researcher conducting a case study. Etic knowledge may be contrasted with emic knowledge or that which is internal to a situation. The pattern of empirical observations at a case study site provides an example of emic knowledge. Given that orthodox case studies rely on propositional knowledge, it may be that they have a greater propensity to start from etic knowledge related to the higher levels of understanding in Llewelyn's framework and use deductive logic to identify propositions that may be examined by studying a case. For example, one statement in the academic literature may be that workers are always dissatisfied when their pay is low compared with workers in similar jobs elsewhere in the area. Another statement in the academic literature may be that organizations whose workers are dissatisfied experience a high level of labour turnover. We may deduce from these two statements that organizations that pay their employees less than that paid to other equally skilled employees in the area will experience higher levels of labour turnover. We may then undertake case study research at a number of organizations to establish whether there is evidence of the relationship between low pay and labour turnover.

By contrast, an emergent case study will have a greater propensity to work from emic knowledge inductively, perhaps using a metaphor to interpret a particular piece of evidence and to build understanding from there. For example, it may be that office workers interact with each other several times each day. A metaphor that might be used is that those workers are like an association football team whose players are often interacting with each other in the course of a match. If we then observe that the office workers' interactions are activities that help them each to complete their respective jobs successfully and that their organization is in direct competition with another organization in their sector, we may conclude that the office workers are in many ways like a football team. We could then proceed to the stage of differentiation to identify ways in which the office team is different from a football team until we can state clearly what constitutes the 'office team' concept to be fitted into explanations or theories about why the team operates as it does. Both an orthodox and an emergent approach may use abductive reasoning by choosing – from a range – the most likely explanation or theory for a piece of evidence.

In order to make a link between a possible explanation and empirical research in a case study, it is necessary to define an applicable unit of analysis – which will be discussed further in Chapter 3 – to which the explanation or theory relates. For example, assume that the context of a case study is an organization. If the research question that is formulated relates to the organization as a whole, the whole organization will be the unit of analysis and data relating to the research question should be collected from anywhere within the organization to help derive an understanding of the case in ways that relate to the research question. If, on the other hand, the research question is about how a particular organizational change affects two specific departments, the focus will be on the change that has taken place and the two departments. Units of analysis then exist at two different levels, namely: (i) the change; and (ii) the two individual departments. Data collection will be directed towards understanding the change and its impact on the two departments. If instead the phenomenon is simply the change and an understanding sought is the nature of the change that is taking place not only in this organization, but at other organizations, the unit of analysis will be the change, but there will be multiple units of analysis of prospective comparable changes at different organizations.

While an orthodox approach will see the definition of the case(s) or unit(s) of analysis taking place in advance of the research data collection process being started, an emergent approach allows the boundaries to the case or the unit of analysis to be defined as the research progresses. However, even in an emergent approach, it is important for both the final research question and the unit of analysis to be defined before the data collection process is completed, to allow the researcher to check that he or she has collected sufficient information from sources that illuminate what is taking place with the unit of analysis to answer the research question which she or he has set.

In this section, we have considered different levels at which theories may be constructed, the types of logic that may be used to link theory to empirical evidence in case studies and the importance of defining the contours to the case when theorizing. The next section discusses different levels of scope for the theories.

DEFINING THE CONTRIBUTION OF THE STUDY

Both Undergraduate and Masters dissertations will be enhanced by the chosen case(s) contributing to the development of theory. When making such a contribution, it is important to define the scope of the theory. In orthodox approaches, a common objective of theorizing about the case that is being observed is to think about the implications that the case may have for elsewhere and how to add to nomothetic knowledge or general statements that have wider applicability. While emergent approaches acknowledge that the theories developed may have implications for elsewhere, this is less of an end *per se* than it is for orthodox approaches. Instead, the focus is upon the particular case and generating ideographic knowledge or explanations of the specific reasons for the phenomenon found in the case. Thus, there are different strategies for defining the scope of the contribution from case study research. In order to understand this, it is necessary to return to the concepts of particularization and generalization.

A strategy of *particularization* seeks to develop deep understanding about the case and explanations that capture the complexity of the case. Any situation, organization or phenomenon that constitutes a case will have its own unique characteristics. These, in turn, will give rise to unique combinations that manifest in a specific phenomenon or a particular manifestation of a broader phenomenon in that case. Particularization entails reporting on why some of the characteristics or events that comprise the case or phenomenon are how they are in the specific context that is being studied. The focus of particularization is to understand and explain the uniqueness of the case. As Stake (1995: 4) says: 'Case study research is not sampling research. We do not study a case primarily to understand other cases. Our first obligation is to understand this one case.'

Stake (1995) suggests that one of the things that arise from a deep understanding is a capacity to recognize when dimensions of the phenomenon appear in new and foreign contexts. This permits what Stake (1995: 7) describes as a *naturalistic generalization*. Generalization is the development of a general statement or proposition by inference of observation of a particular manifestation of a phenomenon or system (Tsang, 2014: 371). Naturalistic generalization is 'arrived at by recognizing the similarities of objects and issues in and out of context and by sensing the natural co-variations of happenings' (Stake, 1995: 7). As some of the researcher's understandings of a previous case may remain tacit and unarticulated, naturalistic generalization to a subsequent case is both intuitive and empirical. Stake (1995: 8) goes on to say that:

> Naturalistic generalizations develop within a person as a product of experience. They derive from the tacit knowledge of how things are, why they are, how people feel about them, and how these things are likely to be later or in other places with which this person is familiar. They seldom take the form of predictions but lead regularly to expectation. They guide action, in fact they are inseparable from action. These generalizations may become verbalized, passing of course from tacit knowledge to propositional; but they have not yet passed the empirical and logical tests that characterize formal (scholarly, scientific) generalizations.

In this regard, it might be that a researcher conducts an emergent case study based on their own workplace and then they observe a similar workplace and find resonance of the same. That would allow them to develop propositional knowledge about both cases.

The development of propositional knowledge would move the naturalistic generalization towards the status of an *analytic* or *theoretical generalization*. As indicated above, orthodox cases tend to seek this type of generalization. Yin (2014) discusses theoretical or analytic propositions that are not generalized statistically to populations – as is sought in quantitative research through probability sampling methods – but which may be generalized to similar situations. Yin (2014: 21) distinguishes between statistical and analytic generalization in suggesting 'in doing a case study, your goal will be to expand and generalize theories (analytic generalization) and not to extrapolate probabilities (statistical generalization)'. Tsang (2014) provides a number of ways in which analytic or theoretical generalization may be developed if one is starting from propositional knowledge. One way is through the practice of *falsification*; that is if an author in the literature has indicated that a proposition has law-like characteristics and that one event always accompanies another, the study and provision of a counter-case would provide a refutation of the universality of the theory. However, simple falsification of an existing theory might not be considered as sufficient by some examiners, even for a Masters dissertation.

There are ways in which case studies can make a more positive contribution even if there is a dimension of falsification of one theory. For example, Tsang (2014: 377) suggests they can be used to *examine the relative merits of different theories* around the same subject and their applicability to particular situations. For example, in the discipline of Change Management, organizational justice theory states that the way employees react to change depends on them being treated fairly. However, within organizational justice theory there is a divergence of views regarding one of the components: interactional justice. One group argues that interactional justice should be considered holistically; the other argues it is perceived by employees as two discrete types of just treatment - treatment of people or interpersonal justice and the explanations provided to them or informational justice. By studying the issue of employees' treatment during a managed change, the two theories can be compared in practice and a choice made.

There are additional ways in which cases may contribute to theoretical generalization (Tsang, 2014: 374). Firstly, they can be used to *extend a theory*. To take the example above, it may be that it has been observed that employees perceived the change had been managed poorly, despite them having been treated justly. However, it could be that the researcher observes that the case study organization was performing poorly and this was not something that had been reported in other cases. In this instance, the extension of the theory from the case study could be that employees' perceptions of their treatment are likely to be influenced by the organization's performance. A second way in which a counter instance could help to develop theory is by *defining boundaries* to a finding. To take the organizational justice example, it may be that all the cases where treatment is considered fair are either public sector or not-for-profit organizations. If the counter finding arises in a commercial, for profit organization, it could be that the boundary to the generalization has been found.

Another form of generalization discussed by Tsang (2014: 371) is that of *empirical generalization*. With an empirical generalization, a number of cases are observed with the purpose of seeing whether there is an empirical regularity or pattern in the population of phenomena or systems from which the cases are drawn; that a pattern is being observed rather than explained. Tsang suggests that the merit of this type of approach is that by identifying a pattern – even if it is not necessarily explained – a specific context may be discounted. The observation or pattern could then become the subject of subsequent theory building. If such an empirical generalization is attempted in a Masters dissertation, you should offer suggestions for the reasons for the pattern in the context of existing literature.

A final form of generalization that might be adopted with case studies is that of *small population generalization*. It may be that a new form of work system is so advanced and expensive that only a small number of organizations have yet to purchase the system. All the organizations with those systems may be known through the trade press making it easy to identify and research all or a high proportion of that population. In this type of instance, it may be possible to generalize the findings relating them to a specific number of that population. Again, the conclusions may simply be empirical to provide the focus for subsequent theory building.

When explaining your research, it is important to express the nature of your contribution - whether it can be considered as common to all institutions of a particular type, to some of that type of institution under specific circumstances, or only to a particular institution – and the limits of that contribution. Thinking about the concepts of different types of generalization and particularization should help you to do this.

SELECTION OF CASES

To theorize successfully about the empirical evidence that has been gathered from the cases studied, it is necessary to consider how those cases fit into the theories that you use or develop. It is, thus, important to consider the rationale for – or ways of selecting – cases. There have been a number of different ways proposed for selecting cases (see for examples, Patton, 2015; Saunders et al., 2016). In outlining the bases for selection, we build on earlier distinctions in relation both to the different case studies of orthodox and emergent and the types of contribution through theorization that might be achieved. Not all the bases of selection are mutually exclusive, nor will their use be confined to either orthodox or emergent case studies, or different forms of contribution, but they may be more associated with one rather than another, which we highlight below.

One approach is that of *opportunistic selection* which will entail picking cases on a basis of on-the-spot decisions about the cases fitting in with the important criteria for the research, or with the new criteria that become apparent in the course of the research. Alternatively, there might be unforeseen opportunities of access to a case that enables the researcher to address the problem under consideration. This type of selection is most likely to be found in emergent case studies and used either for particularization or developing a naturalistic generalization. Many people reading for a Masters degree are either studying part-time because they are in full-time work, or are studying full-time after being awarded sabbatical leave from work. It may be that there is a problem in their workplace that they have always wanted to dedicate time to resolving. The requirement to write a dissertation might provide them with the time to address such a problem and the willingness of their work colleagues might provide them with the opportunity to do so. This type of situation will constitute an opportunistic form of selection.

A second approach is that of *extreme* or *deviant case selection*. Extreme or deviant cases are selected because they are unusual or extreme and offer the potential to learn most either in a positive or a negative way. To some extent, to define a case as extreme or deviant is to accept a realist ontology and positivist epistemology that allow cases to be identified as part of a wider population and to define a norm for a case which allows others to be defined as deviant. By contrast, a constructivist ontology and interpretivist epistemology could lead to an assumption that all cases will be different rendering the idea of deviance invalid. Nevertheless, if the idea of extreme or deviant is accepted, they could be used to illuminate explanations of why a particular case is performing well or badly and provide opportunities for particularization in the explanation.

A third approach is a variant of the idea of an extreme case and that is the *politically important case selection*. This involves choosing cases that are politically sensitive as they allow illumination of particular types of problems that are also considered to be manifest elsewhere, but have come to light in a particularly damaging way in the politically important case. The dangers of an overly close relationship between a firm and its auditors, such as that which occurred at the American energy, commodities and services company Enron in the late 1990s is a particular instance of this. Again, the opportunities for particularization in the explanation of why such a relationship developed in the way that it did at Enron are considerable, although drawing comparisons between Enron and other companies would require some analytic generalization.

A fourth approach is that of *criterion selection*. This involves identifying criteria in advance that distinguish cases from others that make up the majority of a population and using those criteria to select cases. A particular way of using this approach in management research would be to investigate one or more companies that had doubled in size or turnover, or that had encountered an unusually high number of industrial relations problems. The opportunities for particularization in the explanation of why an organization's performance materialized in this way are extensive, although drawing comparisons between the company that meets the criterion and others that did not would require some analytic generalization about the absence of the level of performance at those other companies.

A fifth approach is that of *theory-based selection*. Theory-based selection is similar to criterion selection, but it involves picking cases on the bases of the recognition of evidence of important theoretical constructs at one or more cases. A common form of use of this method in management research is that of early adopters – or innovators – of a particular management practice. The concept of innovators is then used to explain the performance of those cases, as well as others who are not innovators, in relation to the wider population. The cases picked and explained will involve a degree of particularization, although there will also be an underlying form of analytic or theoretical generalization that expresses the way that the cases relate to the wider population.

A sixth approach is that of *snowball* or *chain selection*. It entails asking people who are knowledgeable of the area or research participants whether they are aware of other cases that fit the selection criteria. The consequence is that the researcher is much more likely to find cases that are information-rich than if they were to select the cases by most other means. This form of selection is perhaps most likely to be used as researchers move from particularization to a naturalistic generalization, although it could also be used for the purpose of developing an empirical generalization.

A seventh approach to selection is that of *census selection* where the aim is to study the entire population. When a population is either new, or may be tightly defined for other reasons, it may be possible to study the entire population of one or a small number of cases. This approach is particularly suitable if the objective is to make a small population generalization, although it could also be used for the purposes of making an empirical or an analytic generalization. A similar type of selection is *homogenous selection*. Homogenous selection involves picking a small sub-group of a wider population, but which have definite shared characteristics or identity, to examine how those characteristics are affected by a particular phenomenon or lead to the development of a phenomenon. This form of selection will be particularly suitable for empirical generalization or analytic generalization.

A ninth approach is that of *intensity selection*. Intensity selection involves picking information-rich cases that exhibit a lot of the qualities of the phenomena that are under consideration. Intensity selection can be particularly valuable at the early stages of developing an analytic generalization as the depth of the information about a case may allow development of explanations of extensive patterns. The study of subsequent cases may be used to extend and refine the analytic generalization and to identify the boundaries to its applicability. Of course, if the research stops with the initial case, the theory of the case will be particularization.

A tenth approach that is suited to the development of analytic generalizations is a *maximum variety* or *heterogeneous selection*. This will entail identifying many different characteristics that are found in the population of cases as a whole. The researcher will then select as many cases as possible with each case having a different configuration of some of the characteristics. For example, organizations could be distinguished on the basis of their size, their patterns of ownership, the sector in which they are situated, their geographical location, etc. The extent to which it is possible to select a wide variety of different cases for a Masters dissertation is questionable, but it may be possible for you to study two or three cases and employ the principle of maximum variety. Any theme that is common across the different cases that were selected will then take on increased importance and could provide the basis for an analytic generalization. Also, if the theme is absent from one of the cases, the absence could provide the basis for developing an explanation of the boundary to the analytic generalization.

Although analytic generalization is not related to statistical generalization, the eleventh approach of *purposeful random selection* involves the statistical logic of choosing cases according to a systematic method that has been predetermined to afford all relevant cases equal chance of inclusion. Advocates of this method claim that it can reduce bias in the selection of cases and enhance the credibility of the generalizations that are made. This, of course, will only apply if all the cases support the analytic generalization. As analytic generalization is not based on frequencies, but on theoretical applicability, any counter cases found in the selection may only be useful if they can be used to contribute to defining the boundaries of the analytic generalization.

A twelfth approach, *stratified purposeful selection*, may be used to help refine an analytic generalization or define its boundaries. Stratified purposeful selection involves identifying distinct clusters of cases within a population systematically and then studying them. For example, it might have been found that all family-owned firms with less than 20 employees are able to function without a formal Human Resource Department because of the ways in which the founding family is able to construct an amenable work environment. The idea could then be extended by choosing a cluster of firms with 25 employees. If the findings from cases from each of the clusters are the same, the analytic generalization will be extended. If the findings from each of the clusters are slightly different, it will provide an opportunity to define the boundaries to the initial propositions in the analytic generalization and extend the analytic generalization by identifying reasons why the findings are different in the two different clusters.

A thirteenth approach is *confirming or disconfirming case selection*. This type of approach fits in with the pursuit of analytic generalization and extending the ideas of the theory or identifying the boundaries to its application. If the case confirms the proposition, the analytic generalization is extended; if the case disconfirms the proposition, a boundary of the analytic generalization is found. If the proposition had claimed to be universal, then the theory has been falsified. A fourteenth approach offers a particular type of confirming or disconfirming case and that is *critical case selection*. Critical case selection involves selecting cases where theoretical propositions lead to the assumption that a phenomenon will either be present or absent. The maxim when selecting a critical case is: If a phenomenon is happening anywhere, it is likely to be here; and if it is not happening here, it is unlikely to be happening anywhere else. If the phenomenon is present, a degree of particularization will have taken place about why phenomenon was likely to be present in the critical case and it will also provide the basis for developing analytic generalization. If the case does not support the proposition, then the proposition will have been falsified.

The fifteenth and final approach to selecting cases that will be considered here – simply because other writers use it, but it should not be used in the design of a Masters dissertation – is that of the typical case. The typical case is not different in notable ways from those others that have been found. If a typical case is found in the course of research, it is likely simply to extend the analytic generalization. However, the usefulness of the typical case is limited. As Stake (1995: 4) says 'The first criterion [of case study selection] should be to maximize what we can learn'. The main use of a typical case would be for illustrative or teaching purposes.

Table 2.2 summarizes the relationship between the strategic choice involving the selection of cases and the best approach to developing a contribution when theorizing having made a particular choice. When deciding on the selection choice, it is important to decide on the amount of time that is available to conduct the data collection stage of the research. It may be that this is limited to only about a month. In such a situation, the capability to adopt one or other of the different selection approaches – for example, stratified random selection – may be precluded. Nevertheless, a decision will remain of whether to opt for a single case, or more than one case. If you are going to adopt an emergent approach, it is more likely that a single case will be selected, although it may be that a subsequent case will be chosen to engage in a form of naturalistic generalization and to offer propositions that might provide the basis for an analytic or theoretical generalization if you are tending towards a positivistic epistemology and/or a realist ontology. If you are adopting an orthodox approach, it is more likely that more than one case will be adopted, although only one case may be selected if the selection is of an extreme or deviant, politically important, criterion, theory-based, intensity or a critical case.

Table 2.2 Relationship between choice of selection approach of cases and the form of theorizing that is most likely to be pursued

Method of selection	Form of theorizing most likely to be pursued
Opportunistic	Particularization
Extreme or deviant	Particularization on the basis of assumption of prior analytic generalization
Politically important	Particularization on the basis of assumption of prior analytic generalization
Criterion-based	Particularization on the basis of assumption of prior analytic generalization
Theory-based	Particularization on the basis of assumption of prior analytic generalization
Snowball or chain	Particularization leading to naturalistic generalization and empirical generalization
Census	Small population and empirical generalization
Homogenous	Empirical generalization and analytic generalization
Intensity	Initial stages of analytic generalization
Maximum variety or heterogeneous	Analytic generalization
Purposeful random	Analytic generalization
Stratified purposeful	Extension of the analytic generalization and definition of its boundaries
Confirming or disconfirming	Extension of the analytic generalization and definition of its boundaries
Critical case	Initial stages of analytic generalization or falsification
Typical case	Best used only for teaching or illustrative purposes

EVALUATING YOUR CASE(S)

When your research is completed, it will be evaluated. It is important to think about the criteria by which the work will be assessed. The idea of what constitutes good research when it is written up links to what has become known as the criteriology debate. Proponents of approaches that tend towards orthodoxy suggest four criteria by which all work should be evaluated. For example, Yin (2014: 45-49) provides four criteria that he believes all case studies should seek to meet. Firstly, there is construct validity which defines how well the construct relates to the empirical reality and facilitates its measurement. Secondly, there is internal validity which relates to the accuracy of description of causal relationships. Thirdly, there is external validity which is the extent to which a finding may be generalized to elsewhere. Fourthly, there is reliability, which is the idea that if another investigator was to follow the same procedures and conduct the same case study as a previous investigator, he or she would replicate the earlier findings and arrive at the same conclusions. It will suffice to say at this point that these different criteria have been criticized - either explicitly or implicitly - by a range of authors from a variety of standpoints (Lincoln and Guba, 1985; Stake, 1995: 4; Tsang, 2014: 370-372). If an orthodox approach is adopted with an underlying positivist epistemology, then these are the criteria you should seek to observe.

They are not, however, suitable for all approaches to case studies. As Johnson et al. (2006: 132) have suggested, there is a need for evaluative criteria to take account of the increasing diversity of research approaches. Johnson and colleagues propose what they describe as contingent criteria which will be dependent on the epistemological and ontological position of the researcher. While the four criteria adopted by Yin and others may be appropriate if the researcher has combined positivist epistemology with realist ontology, other criteria will be more appropriate for alternative epistemological and ontological approaches. If the research embodies an interpretivist epistemology, the evaluation criteria will include credibility of the account in place of construct validity, evidence of reflexivity in place of internal validity, transferability or the extent of applicability in place of external validity and confirmability through the researcher's own self-criticism and a clear audit trail in place of reliability. If the research embodies constructivist ontology, the evaluation criteria will include the evidence of multiple voices removing the researcher from the centre of the account.

SUMMARY

This chapter has introduced a number of considerations that are involved in a case study research strategy or the strategic choices that are involved in conducting a case. It has organized those considerations or choices around the classifications of orthodox and emergent cases that were introduced in Chapter 1. We have proceeded through an outline of the underlying philosophies of the different approaches through consideration of levels of theorization and the linkage of those theoretical ideas to empirical evidence through different types of logic. Consideration has been given to the scope of a theory through the concepts of different types of generalization and particularization. We have identified different ways of selecting cases to help build an explanation and we have suggested ways in which cases may be evaluated. Table 2.3 summarizes these considerations and choices.

Table 2.3 Summary of different aspects of orthodox and emergent approaches

	Orthodox	Emergent
Assumptions of design of case – see Chapter 1	Quasi-experimental	Naturalistic
Underlying philosophy	Primarily positivist and realist, although potentially interpretivist and realist	Tendency towards constructivist and interpretivist although also realist and interpretivist
Perceived relationships of concepts to empirical reality	Tendency to view as either a single or one of many possible interpretations or representations of external reality	Tendency to view as either one of many possible interpretations or representations of external reality or one of many possible accounts of reality that has been constructed
Source of initial knowledge	Etic	Emic
Type of logic employed to build theory	Primarily deductive or abductive	Primarily inductive or abductive
Type of knowledge sought	Probably nomothetic	Probably ideographic
Objective of theorizing or contribution from case(s)	Primarily theoretical or empirical generalization	More likely to be particularization, but different forms of generalization possible
Basis of selection of cases	Potential for analytic generalization	Probably particularization
Criteria for evaluation	Positivist criteria to help ensure consistency and generalizability across cases	Contingent

In the next chapter, the components of case study data collection methods are introduced.

3

BASIC COMPONENTS OF CASE STUDIES

INTRODUCTION

The aim of this chapter is to outline and provide an understanding of the basic components of case study research outlined in Chapter 1. We therefore assume that, having read Chapters 1 and 2, you have decided that a case study is likely to be suitable for your research and now need to start thinking about it in more detail. Building on Figures 1.1 and 1.2, we note that, whilst the components are similar within orthodox and emergent case study approaches, their operationalization and use (discussed in Chapter 4) differs when using each of these case study approaches. This chapter starts by considering the components: 'review literature' and 'define research question(s)'. We consider next the 'design study' component. This is followed by a comparison of the 'prepare for study' component in orthodox approaches and the 'collect data' component in emergent approaches emphasizing the similarities and differences between them. We then consider data collection contrasting the 'collect data' component of the orthodox approach with the 'prepare for further study and collect more data' of the emergent approach. Finally, we outline the 'analyse data' and 'write up and report findings' components. Given the book's focus on collecting data we pay particular attention to the first four components.

REVIEW LITERATURE *AND* DEFINE RESEARCH QUESTION(S)

Within the orthodox linear model 'review literature and define research questions' are treated as one component, whereas within the emergent model, whilst interrelated they are treated separately. This distinction is crucial as it emphasizes differences in the role of the literature in developing your research question. Techniques for generating research ideas are outlined in many Business and Management research methods texts (for example, Bryman and Bell, 2015; Saunders et al., 2016). However, what is discussed less widely is how the research question is developed and refined from these initial ideas and the role of the literature review within this. This is particularly crucial, and is discussed in relation to both models in Chapter 4. Whichever model is being used, the key aspect of 'define research question(s)' is to ensure that a case study is appropriate for your particular research project, when compared to alternative research options. This will depend on the research idea and the research question or questions that need to be answered, alongside more practical issues such as gaining access to one or more research sites that are suitable for addressing these questions.

Whether focussing upon the individual phenomenon or institutional level, case study research is particularly useful in answering 'How?' and 'Why?' questions (see Table 3.1), where the understandings and explanations sought are likely to require extensive and in-depth investigation of the nature and complexity of a current phenomenon or phenomena in a real-life setting. Your decision to definitely use a case study is therefore based on your assessment that it will enable you to answer the research question or questions. This does not constrain you to using particular data collection techniques or using only qualitative data, although this will be the dominant data type. Rather, in both orthodox and emergent case study approaches the researcher is looking to answer their research question by understanding and/or explaining in detail the linkages between different aspects of what is happening. She or he will not however be manipulating or intervening in the case study sites (usually one or more organizations in management research) while the research is being carried out.

Research questions and levels at which explanation will be developed

Case studies addressing research questions that focus upon institution level explanations, rather than conceptualization of individual phenomenon, primarily consider an issue or problem within a particular group or organization. For example, Questions 1 and 2 (see Table 3.1) emphasize the institution being studied by placing it first, indicating the researcher is conceiving the research at the level of the institution.

For case study research at the institutional level of understanding, questions are likely to emphasize either a group, an organization or a number of similar organizations such as those in a sector in which the particular types of phenomena of interest are manifest. If we consider the first and second questions in Table 3.1, for each the focus is on a particular organization. For Question 1 the focus is on Organization ABC (the institution) and the reasons why that organization's employees' motivation is

Table 3.1 Examples of 'How?' and 'Why' explanatory research questions that could be answered using case studies

	Question	Level of understanding	Likely nature of case
1	Why at Organization ABC is employees' motivation low?	Institution	Emergent, followed by orthodox
2	How have major high street banks responded to changes in lending regulations in their lending interactions with small business customers?	Institution	Emergent
3	Why is knowledge shared collaboratively for some specialist manufacturing projects, rather than all the work being 'in house'?	Phenomenon	Orthodox

low (the phenomenon) within that institution. This question starts with a particular premise that employees' motivation is low. Through using a case study to answer such 'why' (as well as 'how') questions, the researcher can gain an in-depth and insightful understanding of the phenomenon being researched within that context rather than just describing what is happening (the incidence). She or he will plan to collect data to allow a rich description to be constructed at the institutional level regarding employees' motivation at that particular organization and the reasons for this. Based upon the description the researcher will hope to be able to offer new insights and understanding within the institution in question. The explanation will be bound to the context of the respective institution in which the case study data were collected and the researcher's theoretical contribution will be through particularization.

Question 2, although focussed upon a sector rather than an individual organization, is still concerned with the institutional level of understanding. For this question, the understanding from the case will be context-bound to a type of institution (major high street banks) in which the phenomenon (lending interactions with small business customers) occurs. Through using a case study approach to answer a 'how' question the researcher will have collected data regarding the responses by major high street banks to changes in lending regulations and small business customers' reactions to these. Once again the explanation will be bound to the institutional context in which these data were collected and the theoretical contribution will be realized through particularization.

Case studies addressing research questions that focus upon phenomenon level explanations to understand concepts - rather than developing institutional level explanations - are concerned with a particular phenomenon such as in Question 3 in Table 3.1. In this question the emphasis is given to the phenomenon being studied by placing it first, indicating the researcher is conceiving the research at the level of the phenomenon. Such questions emphasize the phenomenon whilst recognizing that it is occurring within a particular context. They therefore seek to offer insights that are applicable to the phenomenon across a range of contexts, the researcher focussing upon using one or more cases to build theory or develop generalizations.

For Question 3 in Table 3.1, the researcher will be interested in finding out about and understanding the phenomenon of sharing knowledge collaboratively. She or he will be interested in the reasons 'why' such knowledge is shared in some situations but not in others. This phenomenon of knowledge sharing will be studied within a specified context, referred to in the question as specialist manufacturing projects. However, the focus will be upon in-depth insightful explanations, relating to the phenomenon of knowledge sharing, which for this question might consider the similarities and differences between the types of project work undertaken collaboratively and 'in-house' and the associated reasons. The emphasis given to the phenomenon being studied by placing it first, indicates the researcher is conceiving the research at the level of the individual phenomenon and is likely to contribute to theory by using generalization.

Although we have not discussed developing explanations at both the institution and individual phenomenon levels within a case study approach, it is worth reiterating that, as we mentioned in Chapter 2, this may be appropriate. For example, it may be that, although your research focusses on the individual phenomenon level of understanding (as in Question 3), in order to gain access to collect data you offer to also provide analysis focussed upon the organizational level. In such instances you would need to undertake analyses at both levels.

Reviewing the literature and orthodox and emergent case study approaches

The way in which the research questions are defined and the use of academic literature within this for both the institution and individual phenomenon levels differs, dependent upon whether the researcher adopts an orthodox or an emergent case study approach. For orthodox approaches to case study research, the knowledge upon which the research question is conceived and the research subsequently planned will be etic, in other words coming from outside the case study, usually the academic literature. The case study will then be used to answer the research question, the plan being to explore propositions developed from, and clearly justified by, the literature reviewed. Such a plan may arise, for example, from the need to better understand an existing theory, such as its application in a new context or its policy implications, or alternatively to consider implications of rival theories. The crucial consideration for such orthodox cases is to ensure that the research question and what is conceived and planned is grounded in the academic literature. This means the researcher needs to review the academic literature critically in relation to the research topic and, on the basis of this, refine the research question as necessary before designing the study, preparing for study/further study and collecting data.

Question 3 in Table 3.1 has been developed from a critical review of the literature on knowledge sharing and collaborative working with a focus upon specialist manufacturing projects and as such provides an example of an orthodox approach.

From reviewing this literature, the researcher will already be clear that, within supply chain research knowledge has been conceptualized as something that is possessed (Grant, 1996), often ignoring the power already existing in supply chains (Halley et al., 2010). She or he will have planned to use such insights from the literature reviewed as a guide to those aspects that are likely to be most fruitful in the subsequent design of the case study research. For example, subsequent to reviewing the literature, the researcher may have chosen to focus in particular on the issue of power in the integration and coordination of knowledge across organizational boundaries (Rebolledo and Nollet, 2011; Matheus et al., 2016) and his or her design will reflect this.

In contrast, Question 1 is posed by organization ABC and so emerges from within the case. However, as you will already know from your studies, it relates to an area – employee motivation – for which there is a vast amount of academic literature, dating back decades to Maslow's (1943) seminal theory of motivation. Given this, much of the knowledge in which the question will be grounded will, as for Question 3, be etic coming from outside the case study organization. Consequently, despite the question emerging from the organization and theorization focussing upon particularization, the case study could be subsequently planned and progressed by adopting an orthodox approach.

The research question in emergent approaches to case study research is, in contrast, likely to begin in a less constrained way and develop and be clarified, refined and focussed as the case study proceeds. This means the researcher is planning to start the case study research before the research question is developed fully and so the outcome is, invariably, more open-ended. The knowledge that is derived is emic, in other words emerging as the case study research is undertaken and will invariably inform the questions asked. Question 2 in Table 3.1 originates from an issue that was raised first specifically by an organization trying to better understand a particular phenomenon manifest within their particular setting. The introduction of new bank lending regulations by the UK Government's Prudent Regulation Authority (HM Treasury, 2015) was highlighted by the trade press as likely to have impacted on the way UK banks lent money to small businesses. However, as these regulations were new, it was unclear how high street banks would adapt their lending criteria or which aspects of the regulations would most affect small business customers. The very recent introduction of these regulations meant there was no academic literature on UK banks' responses at the time of this research. This is not to say that the academic literature was unimportant in planning this, as in other emergent case studies; only that the research question was not derived from it. Indeed, a Google Scholar search had highlighted that different banks concentrated their lending on different SME sectors (Gray et al., 2013), and this was incorporated in the subsequent design by including multiple units of analysis (high street banks) within the overall institutional case.

Invariably, for orthodox model case studies, as more literature is read the research question will become more clearly defined, particular articles and book chapters suggesting ways in which the question can be more tightly specified. Similarly, for emergent case studies, as the case study research progresses, your ideas will become clearer as you understand the case more fully and these will be informed by the literature. We believe it is important to note both the specific idea and the reasoning; including references to specific articles and new knowledge that you discover about the case that inform your research questions and subsequent stages of the research. We recommend this is done as soon as possible after having the idea as it is all too easy to forget the precise argument. For this reason, we strongly recommend you keep a research notebook in which you record chronologically all aspects of your research throughout the research project. Your research notebook is likely to be an important resource for other components of the case study approach, including designing the study, which we consider below.

DESIGN STUDY

The design study component is concerned with developing a justified overall case study framework for the collection and subsequent analysis of data to answer the research question, be it emerging or fully formed. It is therefore concerned with the overall plan for your case study research rather than the finer details such as the precise themes that will be covered in your interviews or exactly how you intend to analyse the data collected. Whilst it may seem obvious that you will undertake your research within a series of real world constraints and requirements, this is something that is often overlooked at the design stage. We consider it crucial to recognize that, as with all research, you develop your research design within the set of constraints that are particular to your situation. You need to recognize the time and resource budgets you have available and the need to stay within these and also meet your Masters programme's assessment criteria. Whilst we trust that you will act ethically when undertaking your research, it is important to begin to think about ethical issues when considering this component. For example, for both orthodox and emergent approaches, there will be a need to ensure that your research design fulfils your university's ethical code or guidelines, those of any organization or organizations you are intending to use as case studies, and those of any professional body of which you are a member. As we discuss below, you also need to begin to consider how you will gain access to the data you intend to collect for your case study and ensure, as far as is practicable, that this will be possible. Remember, a rigorous research design is of little use if you are unable to gain access to collect data.

Your study design takes as its starting point the research question and whether the explanation will be developed at the institutional level, the individual phenomenon level, or at both levels. As part of this you will need to consider whether you intend to theorize through the particular or by generalizing. Research design then considers in overview what you need to do to enable the research question to be answered within the context of the time and resources available and, crucially, allowing your course assessment criteria to be met. It is in effect a justified outline of what you intend to do, and for many universities is required as part of a research proposal. Like all research designs, this component needs to offer clear reasoned justifications (Saunders et al., 2016) for the research question, the data you intend to collect and the proposed methods of data collection and techniques you will use to analyse these data. Of course, if you are conducting an emergent approach, you will elaborate on these details as your research progresses. Your justifications should, where appropriate, be supported by reference to the academic literature. In offering and justifying a framework to answer the research question, the design component therefore needs, within the specific research context, to outline:

1. The research question, be it emergent or fully formed, and how for the former this will be clarified as the case study develops;
2. Whether, as discussed in the previous section, the resultant understandings and explanations will relate to the institution, the phenomenon or both levels and the nature of associated theorization;
3. The unit(s) at which analysis is undertaken;
4. The data that are likely to be required to enable this theorization at the proposed level(s) and unit(s) of analysis and;
5. In overview, the sources from which these data are likely to be obtained.

Below, we consider the last three of these issues - i.e., the unit(s) at which analysis will be undertaken, the data required and how they will be obtained.

Unit of analysis

Case study research designs, particularly those using an orthodox approach, are often presented using Yin's (2014) four-fold typology. This is based on two dimensions: (i) unit of analysis - holistic or embedded and (ii) number of cases - single or multiple. A *holistic single case design* involves one case study that is analysed as one whole unit. In contrast a *holistic multiple case design* involves two or more case studies each of which are analysed separately as whole units. An *embedded single case design* involves conducting the analysis for two or more sub units that occur within a single case study. Finally, for an *embedded multiple case design*, analysis is conducted on each of the sub units occurring in two or more case studies. Yin's typology therefore emphasizes the need to consider the number of case studies that will be undertaken and how these case studies will be analysed. What it does not do is relate the design to the level at which the explanation will be developed, in other words whether the focus is the individual phenomenon (conceptualization) or the institution in which that phenomenon is manifest (context bound).

In Chapter 2 we considered, albeit briefly, case study design and in particular the unit of analysis in relation to the level at which the explanation would be developed, in other words the level at which theorization would be developed. Within this we highlighted how, at the institutional level, analysis could take place for both a single overall case and also for each of a number of cases embedded in the institution. We also noted that at the individual phenomenon level of explanation, analysis could take place for a single case or for multiple cases. The three columns in Figure 3.1 represent these units of analysis: single, embedded and multiple cases.

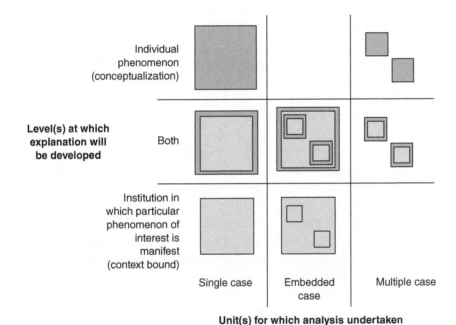

Figure 3.1   Levels of explanation and unit(s) of analysis

Case study designs addressing research questions that focus upon institutional level explanations, rather than conceptualization of individual phenomenon are most likely to use either single or embedded case designs. For case studies planned using an orthodox approach to develop explanation at the institutional level, the choice of a single case as the unit of analysis reflects a need to only understand the phenomenon at the level of the whole organization, associated theorization being likely to be at the particular. Consequently, if – as for research Question 1 (see Table 3.1) – the focus is only on employee's motivation at organization ABC then a single case design will be employed and the data collected will be to understand the reasons for their motivation. In contrast, for an emergent case study design such as Question 2, what may commence as a single case with one unit of analysis - the high-street bank – may metamorphose into an embedded case as more is discovered. For this question the researcher initially designed the study to consider major high street banks' responses as a whole. Subsequently as data were collected it became apparent that, although there had been a tightening of lending requirements by all banks, individual high street banks were responding in different ways regarding their lending to particular market segments and in the information they provided to potential small business customers. As a consequence, the research design was amended to allow analysis for both embedded units (individual banks) and these grouped together as a single unit (major high street banks). This allowed theorization at the institutional level that took into account differential responses to the changes in regulations and the reasons for this.

Case study designs addressing research questions that focus upon explanations of an individual phenomenon are more likely to comprise either a single case or multiple cases. We have already seen that for Question 3 (see Table 3.1), following a review of the literature, the researcher may have chosen to focus on the role of power within knowledge integration across organizational boundaries when looking at knowledge sharing in specialist manufacturing projects. For this research she or he may design a study to look in depth at the phenomenon through one particular manufacturing project, the data collected relating to this particular project. If this were undertaken, the design would be a single case study, although the aim would be to generalize, offering theorization that was applicable across a range of contexts rather than the one project. Alternatively, if the researcher decided to focus on the phenomenon in depth by researching two or more distinct manufacturing projects and analysing the data from each of the cases separately to allow comparisons between contexts, this would be a multiple case design. Once again the aim would be to generalize, offering theorization about the phenomenon, sharing knowledge that was applicable across a range of contexts. In this multiple case design the number of cases would be dependent, in part, on the comparisons that the literature indicated would be fruitful and the resources available. For an emergent approach focussing upon an individual phenomenon the research may commence by looking at a single case but evolve into a multiple case study as more insights are uncovered. These subsequent cases might, particularly where time was limited, gravitate to being more orthodox in their approach.

Although we have not discussed combining all three units of analysis within a case study approach, we note that this may be appropriate when combining individual and phenomenon levels of analysis. For example, it may be that, although your research focuses on the individual phenomenon level of understanding, as in Question 3, in order to gain access to collect data you offer to also provide analysis focussed upon the organizational level for each of the case study organizations. In such instances, you might choose to undertake analyses for each organization as a multiple case and embed them in the overall phenomenon. This is represented by the central square in Figure 3.1.

Data required

The data required invariably depends upon the research question(s) and the nature of theorizing. For emergent research questions, you will, as we outline in Chapter 4, be unable to specify precisely what data are required at the start of your research. However, as your research progresses – and as you understand your case or cases and the institution or phenomenon you are researching – your research question will become clearer and more tightly defined. For orthodox case studies, your research question will be well defined before you commence data collection. This means you should be able to work out precisely what data you will require to answer it. In these instances, previous research you have considered as part of your literature review is likely to indicate those data most likely to be useful in answering your research questions.

Sources of data

Case study research makes use of multiple sources of data to provide evidence within the one case study to develop as rich an understanding as possible (Yin, 2014). It is therefore likely that the research will involve combinations of both secondary and primary data sources, their relative utility depending on the case study model adopted and the associated objective for theorization (Box 3.1). Primary data sources will involve you in designing the collection procedures and collecting your own data and can often be time consuming. For Masters dissertations that are, by their nature time limited, it is worth noting that secondary data sources can, as the data have already been collected for a different purpose, provide longitudinal evidence where these data have been collected over an extended period of time. We discuss both primary and secondary sources below when we consider the 'prepare for study' and 'collect data' components.

PREPARE FOR STUDY AND COLLECT DATA

Chapter 2 highlighted the differences between the orthodox linear approach and the emergent approach for case studies. Whilst both emphasize the need to prepare for study/further study, the initial preparation process is of a more iterative nature in the emergent approach and incorporates initial data collection. Literature outlining the orthodox approach emphasizes the desirability of developing a case study protocol that along with an overview of the research contains the data collection procedures, actual questions that will be used to collect the data and a guide regarding how the research will be reported (Yin, 2014). Whilst this at first glance seems similar to the research proposal outlined in the previous section, key differences are: the inclusion of the actual data collection questions (see Box 3.1), guidance regarding how you will introduce the research to intended participants and build rapport, and reference to potential ethical issues. Whilst it may be possible to develop the list of questions or interview prompts in an orthodox approach, this is unlikely to be either possible or desirable for an emergent approach (Stake, 1995). Rather these will emerge as the research progresses. Despite this, for both approaches there is a need to ensure a number of aspects are addressed prior to commencing data collection. These relate to ensuring you have the relevant skills, access negotiation and the need to begin to understand the case study or studies being researched, the need for ethical approval and to think through the data sources and collection procedures that are likely to be of most use. Whilst these are invariably presented in an ordered way, it is worth noting that the work you undertake for each of these aspects as part of your preparation is interrelated and iterative, involving you in revisiting each of these aspects a number of times (Saunders et al., 2016).

Box 3.1   Outline case study protocol[1]

This is an outline – the actual protocol would go into greater detail in all sections.

TITLE OF RESEARCH PROJECT:

An exploration of collaborative knowledge sharing in specialist manufacturing projects.

OVERVIEW OF THE CASE STUDY:

(justification for the research and research objectives)

This study investigates the influence of power on knowledge integration in innovation projects in supply chains. Such knowledge integration is a major issue for product innovation and manufacture across intra- and inter-organizational boundaries (Rebolledo and Nollet, 2011). Studies examining knowledge integration, knowledge transfer or knowledge sharing in supply chains have tended to adopt the knowledge-as-possession view (Kogut and Zander, 1992; Nonaka, 1994; Grant, 1996). This has been criticized for ignoring power existing in firms (Foucault, 1980) and supply chains (Halley et al., 2010; Matheus et al., 2016).

Such omissions highlight the need for a multidimensional conceptualization of power and the need for research to address three questions:

1   What elements of dimensions of power facilitate supply chain knowledge integration in supply chains?
2   How do these elements of power facilitate supply chain knowledge integration and what are their interrelationships (if any)?

DATA COLLECTION:

(gatekeeper/contact(s) and issues of access, primary and secondary data collection techniques, ethical issues including consent)

Physical access has been granted by Organization DEF (Contact: Mr Andy Other, a.other@organizsationdef.com; 0123-45678910), an original equipment manufacturer and initial contact made with the associated supply chain organizations two of whom have also agreed to participate. These are Supplier123 (Contact: Ms Yasmin E. Tanother, y.e.tanother@supplier123.com; 01987-6543210) and Supplier456 (Contact: Mr Lyon A. Stone, l.a.stone@supplier456.co.uk; 01987-77665544).

Participants currently involved in product innovation projects and associated inter-organizational activities will be identified using snowball sampling. Each will be provided with an information sheet detailing the project, assurances of anonymity and confidentiality and their right to withdraw at any time. Following an explanation of the project and the answering of any questions they will be asked verbally if they wish to participate. If they consent to participate they will be asked to sign a consent form.

An overview of the organization and the two associated supply chain organizations will be obtained from these organizations' websites. Copies of each of the organizations' annual reports have already been downloaded. Access will be sought for associated internal documentation where this is considered appropriate. This is likely to include reports, scorecards and business process documents. However, at this stage it is unclear precisely what documentation will be made available.

Data will be collected using audio recorded semi-structured interviews and will be conducted with those currently involved in product innovation projects and associated inter-organizational activities.

KEY DATA COLLECTION QUESTIONS:

An interview checklist will be used for each interview. This may be amended after each interview dependent on the information received and the need to probe emergent avenues of inquiry.

Thank participant for agreeing to take part

Ensure that they are aware of project, what is involved in participation, have received a consent form and that they're still willing to take part

Ask them to sign the consent form

(Continued)

Please outline a successful innovation project in which you have been involved

[Prompt for] internal interactions with other people/departments/sections within Organization DEF

[Prompt for] external interactions with other people/departments/sections with Supplier 123 and Supplier 456

[Prompt for] external interactions with other people/departments/sections with Supplier 123 and Supplier 456

[Prompt for] project requirements and activities

[Prompt for] process improvement activities

[Prompt for] conflict situations and how resolved

[Prompt for] decision making processes

[... further interview questions and prompts would follow]

REQUIREMENTS FOR DISSERTATION AND ANY SUMMARY REPORTS FOR ORGANIZATIONS *(details from assessment criteria such as word length, structure, use of academic literature, use of primary and secondary data, recommendations for practice, deadline dates set by university and/or organization, etc.):*

This will be dependent upon your university and what you have promised the organization, for example, a summary report.

REFERENCES *(full list of references used in protocol in Harvard format):*

Foucault, M. (1980) *Power/knowledge: selected interviews and other writings, 1972-1977.* Brighton: Harvester Press.

Grant, R. (1996) Prospering in dynamically-competitive environments: Organizational capability as knowledge integration. *Organization Science,* **7**, 375-387.

Halley, A., Nollet, J., Beaulieu, M., Roy, J. and Bigras, Y. (2010) The impact of the supply chain on core competencies and knowledge management: directions for future research. *International Journal of Technology Management,* **49**, 297-313.

Kogut, B. and Zander, U. (1992) Knowledge of the firm, combinative capabilities, and the replication of technology. *Organization Science,* **3**, 383-397.

Matheus, T., Saunders, M.N.K. and Chakraborty, S. (2016 online first) Multiple dimensions of power influencing knowledge integration in supply chains, *R&D Management*, DOI: 10.1111/radm.12243.

Nonaka, I. (1994) A dynamic theory of organizational knowledge creation. *Organization Science*, **5**, 14-37.

Rebolledo, C. and Nollet, J. (2011) Learning from suppliers in the aerospace industry. *International Journal of Production Economics*, **129**, 328-337.

[1]Developed with support from Thomas Matheus

Relevant skills

Within his text on case studies, Yin (2014: 73) emphasizes the importance of the researcher having the necessary skills to undertake case study research. He argues that these relate primarily to your abilities to being able to conduct qualitative interviews and in particular your questioning and listening skills and your ability to 'stay adaptive' that is be open to new situations as opportunities for further data collection. We will look at the operationalization of these research skills when we explore how to collect data in Chapter 4. However, it is worth emphasizing that case study data collection comprises more than just interviewing as it also includes other primary data collection techniques such as observation and questionnaires as well as incorporating secondary data such as organization's records (Farquhar, 2012). What is important at the preparation stage is that you give some thought to the skills that you are likely to need to undertake a case study and, where you do not have these, have a plan regarding how they can be developed.

Access

Almost all case study data collection for Masters dissertations is undertaken in one or more organizations; consequently, your ability to negotiate access will be crucial to your case study research. The access required is dependent upon what is practicable or feasible, the need to be able to collect sufficient data to answer your research question and, of equal importance, what will be acceptable to the institution or institutions from which you are intending to collect data.

Invariably case study research, in seeking to obtain data that will give in-depth insights, requires access that may be considered by some potential participants to be intrusive. In such situations, even though a gatekeeper or broker may have granted physical access to a case study organization, you will still need to gain cognitive access to individual participants. Even the best research design will not work without access to data and so you will rely on what is possible. Buchanan et al. (2013: 53-54) summarize this noting:

> Fieldwork is permeated with the conflict between what is theoretically desirable on the one hand and what is practically possible on the other ... members of organizations block access to information, constrain the time allowed for inter-views, lose your questionnaires, go on holiday and join other organizations in the middle of your unfinished study. In this conflict between the desirable and the possible, the possible always wins.

For both orthodox and emergent approaches to case study research, physical access will need to have been granted prior to data collection. Even if you are planning to use an organization for which you work or with which you are familiar, it is crucial that you seek and obtain formal permission to undertake your research. Such permission is, however, unlikely to be sufficient on its own to allow collection of data that offers in-depth insights in relation to the research question. Rather individual participant's trust and consent to be involved in the research will be needed. The gaining of such cognitive access is an ongoing process after physical access has been granted (Marshall and Rossman, 2011). In addition, for emergent models of research it is also likely to be incremental as research questions are redefined and refined on the basis of insights gained from data already collected.

Understanding the case study or case study institutions

Within Chapter 2, we outlined a series of 15 ways of selecting cases to answer the research question, albeit a question that may be only partially formed for emer-gent cases. These were summarized in Table 2.2, which highlighted the relationship between the selection approach and the form of theorizing that is most likely to be used to make a contribution. The justification for selection, using one or a combina-tion of these reasons, necessitates at least a basic knowledge of potential case study institutions from which the selection will be made. Fortunately, such basic information is often available by undertaking an online search for the organization. Such informa-tion is also useful in helping facilitate access as at least a basic level of familiarity signals to the gatekeeper an interest in the prospective case study or studies, and that the researcher has thought carefully about the research.

Ethical approval

Within this chapter we have already alluded to the need to seek and obtain formal eth-ical approval prior to data collection and how, in many universities, it is an essential component of all research projects. In the context of case study research, ethical approval will be based on how the research will be conducted with regards to the rights of those who are involved in the research or affected by it. What is likely to be considered ethical, and what is unethical, will be set out in your university's ethical code of practice, guidelines or statements of research practice. In addition, if you are a member of a professional association or institute you are likely to have to also abide by their code of practice. However, such codes tend to be written in abstract terms with a focus upon preventing misconduct (Bell and Bryman, 2007). As a consequence, it is necessary for you to interpret the standards and ensure they are not transgressed by the particular case study research design when submitting your research for formal approval. It is also worth noting that some institutions, notably those involved with healthcare and children, have their own specific ethical approval processes, which also need to be met formally prior to undertaking research.

Whilst formal approval is obviously important, acting ethically throughout the research process is an essential component of good case study research (McAreavey and Muir, 2011). Acting ethically is based on a series of ethical principles that need to be adhered to throughout all components of both orthodox and emergent case study approaches (see Table 3.2). Whilst these appear to be related in the main to primary data – data collected specifically for the research project – it is important to recognize that ethical issues also apply to data originally collected for some other purpose. This is particularly apparent when considering such secondary data that are not available publicly. In such instances, it is important that express permission is obtained to use such data.

Table 3.2 Ethical principles and associated issues for different components of case study research

Principle	Illustrative ethical behaviour	Components where often most evident
Integrity of researcher	Acting openly and being truthful	All
Respect for others	Recognizing rights of those participating (see below)	Design study, Collect data, Analyse data, Write up and report findings
Privacy of participants	Ensuring the privacy of those who take part	Collect data, Analyse data, Write up and report findings
Avoidance of harm (non-maleficence)	Avoiding embarrassment, stress, discomfort, pain Avoiding harassing potential participants to take part Violating assurances of confidentiality or anonymity	Collect data, Analyse data, Write up and report findings
Confidentiality of participants	Ensuring that the researcher does not reveal (keeps secret) the identity of participants to others	Collect data, Analyse data, Write up and report findings

(Continued)

Table 3.2

Principle	Illustrative ethical behaviour	Components where often most evident
Anonymity of participants	Ensuring participant's identity cannot be linked to their specific responses	Collect data, Analyse data, Write up and report findings
Informed consent	Ensuring the participant fully understands the research and the researcher abides by what has been agreed, re-seeking consent for any amendments	Collect data, Analyse data, Write up and report findings
Voluntary nature of participation	Ensuring the right to withdraw both during and after data collection	Collect data, Analyse data, Write up and report findings
Compliance with data protection legislation	Ensuring compliance with legal requirements for managing research in the country or countries in which research is conducted	Analyse data, Write up and report findings
Ensuring researcher safety	Ensuring research design does not cause harm to the researcher such as by placing them in an unsafe situation	Collect data

Data sources and collection procedures

Data sources and collection procedures are outlined below in the next section of this chapter and their operationalization illustrated in Chapter 4. However, likely data sources can be identified as part of the preparation component. Even for emergent models, Stake (1995: 56) notes that selection of data sources can be left too much to chance arguing the researcher should have a 'connoisseur's appetite for the best persons, processes and occasions'. Within this he argues that best refers to those that will enable the researcher to most fully understand the case. Whilst the data sources that present themselves in one situation may be different to those that are available in another situation, and no two cases will be the same, it still makes sense to think of from whom it would be appropriate to collect data, what method or methods of data would be most suitable and when it would be appropriate to collect such data.

Case study research makes use of a variety of data sources and collection procedures to provide evidence within the case study allowing as rich an understanding as possible (Stake, 1995; Yin, 2014). It is therefore likely that the research will involve combinations of a number of primary and secondary data sources; their relative utility depending on the case study model adopted and the associated form of theorization (see Table 3.3).

Table 3.3 Case study approaches, theorization and indicative data collection procedures and sources

Case study approach	Objective of theorization leading to contribution	Evidence*	Indicative secondary data sources	Indicative primary data collection procedures
Orthodox	Generalization	Qualitative	Organization reports/ archival records/ documentation	Interviews, Group interviews, Focus groups, Participant observation, Diaries
		(Quantitative)	Organization databases/surveys, Market research and industry reports, Open access databases	Questionnaires, Structured observations
Emergent	Particularization	Qualitative	Organization reports/archives/ documentation	Interviews, Group interviews, Focus groups, Participant observation, Diaries
		(Quantitative)	Organization databases/surveys	Questionnaires
	(Generalization)	Qualitative	Organization reports/ archival records/ documentation	Interviews, Group interviews, Focus groups, Participant observation, Diaries
		(Quantitative)	Organization databases/surveys, Market research and industry reports, Open access databases	Questionnaires

*Brackets signify lower frequency of use

Secondary data sources that could be appropriate, depending upon the research question, include organizations' internal documentation, reports and information held in organizational databases; as well as items that are readily accessible via the Internet such as organizational web pages, news reports relating to the organization and Facebook pages providing insights to support particularization (see Table 3.3). Whilst for both orthodox and emergent case study approaches it may not be possible to know precisely what secondary data are available within an organization prior to commencing the fieldwork, consideration in advance of those sources likely to be available may be helpful in subsequent requests for access to potential data. Data sources external to the organization can provide useful contextual background evidence as well as supporting evidence for subsequent generalization. However, because such data were collected originally for a different process they may not match your research question precisely.

Primary data comprises that evidence collected specifically for the research project, and so can involve a wide variety of data collection procedures including observation, interviews and questionnaires (see Table 3.3). Their use therefore allows precise focussing on the research question and, for emergent case studies, amendments to be made as the research evolves. Although these procedures are discussed in more detail below and their operationalization outlined in Chapter 4, it is worth noting that those used most widely in case study research are those which inform understanding and interpretation, that is, observation and interviews, in particular participant observation and semi-structured and unstructured interviews (Farquhar, 2012). These procedures, unlike questionnaires, which support measurement by collecting information about the same constructs from a large number of respondents, offer the opportunity to begin to understand the complexity of a phenomenon in a real-life setting. Their semi or unstructured nature allows interesting lines of enquiry to be pursued as they arise.

COLLECT DATA

The collect data component comprises obtaining of evidence to enable the research question to be answered. It includes obtaining appropriate secondary data from identified sources and the collection of primary data using appropriate procedures both from within and external to the organization (see Table 3.4). The precise choice of data sources and collection procedures will depend on the research question being answered. However, it is worth noting that most case studies make use of more than one data source and method. Where two or more qualitative methods are combined or, alternatively two or more quantitative methods are used in combination Tashakkori and Teddlie (2010) refer to this as *multi-method studies*. Where both qualitative and quantitative methods are used in combination they term this *mixed methods studies*.

Table 3.4   Selected data sources and collection procedures for case studies

Data type	Within organization	External to the organization
Secondary	Organization databases/existing surveys, Organization archival records/ reports/ documentation	Market research and industry reports, Open access databases
Primary	Interviews, Group interviews, Focus groups, Participant observation, Diaries, Questionnaires, Structured observations	

Within organization secondary data

Within organization secondary data comprise of both raw data, where there has been little, if any processing, and compiled data that have already been summarized. *Raw data* includes data held in organization databases that have originally been collected for some other purpose such as that collected both routinely and on an ad-hoc basis to support particular functions such as marketing, human resource management and finance. It therefore includes individual employee records, details of customers and their purchasing patterns and the like, as well as the data from organizational surveys such as those generated by employee attitude or customer satisfaction questionnaires. Such secondary data are invariably only available where access is granted by the organization. They can be re-analysed, often statistically, to provide quantitative evidence. Raw secondary data also includes that held in organizations' archives such as minutes of meetings, copies of emails and letters and the like as well as copies of reports and documents such as those detailing processes and procedures. Once again use of such data is dependent upon access being granted, subsequent analysis of predominantly non-numeric data being undertaken to generate quantitative evidence.

Compiled data are often found in organizational documents produced as part of the functioning of the organization. Such documents include, amongst others, reports to shareholders, the text and pictures of organizational web pages, and summary reports produced from data collected during organizational surveys. Where these documents are already available publicly, the information they contain can normally be used without seeking permission. However, if there is any doubt we advise you to obtain permission.

External to the organization secondary data

Secondary data that are sourced external to the organization have usually already been compiled in some way. These data may relate specifically to one aspect of the organization such as share prices over a particular time period, that have been aggregated into a table in the financial pages of a national newspaper and presented alongside those of other traded companies. More generally, such data are available online through subscription services to online databases, often accessed through your business school or your university's library. These contain a wide variety of corporate information such as real time financial data. Secondary sources that are external to an organization are also provided for a sector, country or some other grouping. Their main use in case study research may be to provide contextual information, particularly when seeking to generate theoretical generalizations. These data include industry, region or country statistics compiled by nations' statistical agencies alongside reports produced by market research companies, industry and professional bodies and national newspapers. While freedom of information legislation has meant the former of these are increasingly available to download free of charge via Internet gateways and national archives, many commercial data providers, for example Bloomberg, are only available by subscription.

Primary data collection procedures

Within your Masters programme you will almost certainly have come across a range of procedures for collecting data. These range from those that are suited to collecting detailed, in-depth data from a relatively small number of participants (semi-structured and unstructured interviews, group interviews, focus groups, participant observation, diaries) to those that are better suited to collecting standardized data from a large number of respondents (questionnaires, structured observation, diaries). We now provide an overview of each, and consider the advantages and disadvantages in relation to case study research.

Semi-structured interviews, rather than having a specified set of questions, comprise a set of themes and associated prompts prepared prior to the interview as a checklist (Cassell, 2015). Whilst these provide the basic structure for an interview with a participant, the order in which they are covered and the precise questions asked will vary depending on the research situation, the interviewer asking new questions as necessary such as to find out more about a new but relevant aspect. They differ from *unstructured interviews* which are less formal and do not have predetermined questions. Both forms of interview allow the topics covered to be focussed precisely on the case study and with careful questioning the revealing of participants' detailed views and associated reasoning and insightful explanations. However, the quality of data obtained depends upon the skill of the interviewer and careful selection of interview participants. Their time-consuming nature also means it is not possible to undertake large numbers of such interviews.

Semi-structured interviews can be conducted face-to-face, by telephone or online, for example using Skype™ or Messenger™. The interviewer's role is to create a situation that encourages the participant to talk about those aspects that are relevant to the research questions. The questions asked therefore need to be phrased in language that will be both understandable and familiar to participants. Within each interview participants can be asked about their understandings and opinions of specific events. They can also be asked about their insights in relation to these events, such as how they felt and the reasons for their feelings. Often responses to questions can be used to develop new questions that are followed up in subsequent interviews. This means it is important to listen carefully throughout the interview. Participants may also volunteer further people whom they consider would be useful for you to interview as part of your research, in effect snowball selection, and suggest possible useful secondary data. Where participants assist in these ways, providing considerable assistance to the research, they are often known as *key informants*. It is important not to become over dependent upon one key informant for data – particularly with orthodox case studies – and to corroborate their data with that from other sources such as secondary data, or acknowledge the uncorroborated nature of controversial claims when writing up your research.

Group interview is a generic term used to describe either semi-structured or unstructured interviews conducted with two or more people (Saunders et al., 2016). Typically, such groups form either naturally, for example, a work group within an organization, or have been manufactured or brought together for the purposes of the research (Cassell, 2015). The latter include *focus group* interviews where a homogenous group of participants take part in a moderated discussion of topics and in which the interactions between these participants is a crucial part of the process. Group interviews and focus groups are argued to produce insightful and useful research data in a reasonable time frame when compared to semi-structured and unstructured interviews. However, the utility of the data collected depends upon the participants selected and the skills of the interviewer or moderator.

At first glance, *group interviews* and *focus groups* appear similar to semi-structured interviews, both using a checklist. However, they are different, not least because of the need for the interviewer to manage within group dynamics such as perceptions of status, possible dominance of certain members and aspects of confidentiality. To minimize these difficulties, Saunders et al. (2016) recommend selecting participants of similar status and work experience. As it is difficult to manage the process and take notes at the same time, we recommend audio recording group interviews. It is important to be clear regarding the reasons for interviewing a group rather than individuals. Thomas (2016) advises that group interviews and focus groups should only be used where the group itself is likely to have an impact on the answers to the research question(s).

Typically, group interviews and focus groups involve between four and twelve participants, the precise number depending upon the nature of the participants, the research question and the skill of the interviewer; larger groups and more complex subjects being more difficult to manage. Like semi-structured interviews, participants are usually chosen purposively, a frequent reason being that the researcher will learn a lot from interviewing this group as they are 'information rich' (Krueger and Casey, 2014: 23). The researcher therefore has to try and ensure all participants contribute. In a group interview the researcher leads the discussion, asking questions of those in the group, which they then answer. In a focus group the researcher's role is different; stimulating or facilitating discussion between participants on the questions on the checklist. Consequently, the researcher's role in the discussion is more marginal in focus groups than group interviews, acting as a moderator.

Participant observation comprises two main forms of observation based on the extent to which the researcher participates within the case study setting. Where a researcher participates fully in the case study setting – such as by working for an organization and at the same time collects data through observation – this is termed *complete participant observation*. For case study research, it is likely that much participant observation will be unstructured enabling the researcher to gain an in-depth understanding of what is happening within the context in which it occurs. Using such unstructured observation, the researcher makes notes to record what is happening in as much detail as possible. However, it is worth noting that observational data can also be collected in a more structured form using a coding schedule, which lists the precise categories and level of detail for which the data will be recorded. Whilst such observations offer the advantage of collecting in-depth data in real time and within context, they are extremely time consuming. In addition, particularly for overt observation, the participants may act differently because they are being observed; this being known as the Hawthorne effect.

Within orthodox case studies observations are more likely to be structured than unstructured, although this depends on the question being answered. Structured

Title of meeting: Observer: Date:	Plan of meeting: A = team member B = team leader C = team member D = team member

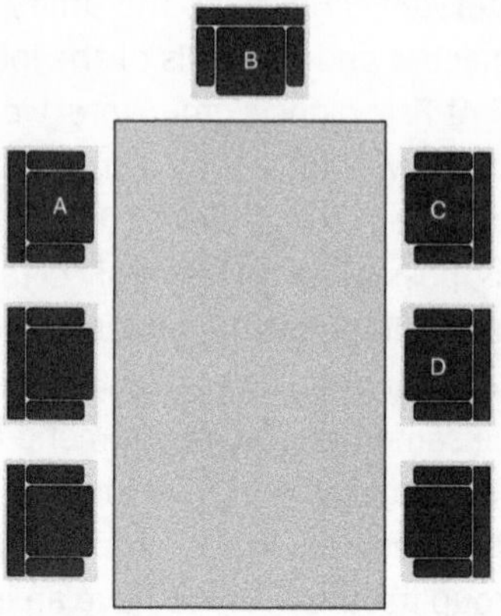

	A	B	C	D
Taking initiative				
Making positive/helpful suggestions				
Drawing in others				
Responding to others				
Showing disagreement in a positive way				
Making negative/unhelpful suggestions				
Clarifying and summarizing				

Additional comments:

Figure 3.2 Structured observation recording sheet for a meeting

observation might involve observation of meetings or processes such as the interaction between a customer and staff member in a fast food restaurant. In undertaking such structured observations, the researcher assumes that what is being observed, such as a meeting, can be broken down into a series of discrete elements that can be assessed. The researcher defines these elements, using the literature reviewed, and following a pilot test of the observation sheet collects data using a recording sheet (see Figure 3.2). This is often undertaken as a passive observer rather than actively taking part.

For unstructured observation in its most extreme form the researcher immerses her or himself fully within the fieldwork situation and, in effect, participates completely. This might include being an employee of an organization, which she or he is observing. Alternatively, it might involve taking part in a particular experience such as backpacking tour of South East Asia. However, such unstructured observations are only likely to take pace in orthodox case studies where such unstructured activity is part of the research question, or where data cannot be accessed through other means. Because the researcher participates as a member of the group she or he comes to understand the world of the informants, allowing a deep and nuanced understanding of their interactions and the associated meanings. For such unstructured observation, it is essential to be clear regarding how the observations will be recorded in the field. Invariably this will be context specific and depend on the role being adopted when observing, for example many people taking part in backpacking tours keep a travel diary or write a blog. Consequently, writing observational field notes may be perceived by others as simply a travel diary. In making such field notes, it is important that these are made close to the actual observation, in order that valuable data are not lost. Often it will subsequently be necessary to word-process hand-written field notes adding other aspects from memory.

In *diary studies*, participants are asked to keep a *diary* recording events and experiences. These can be recorded at specific times at varying levels of frequency depending on the research question, ranging from hours through days to weeks or months. Alternatively, data can be recorded only when specified events occur. The amount of structure imposed on those keeping a diary can also vary considerably, ranging from a free-flowing format to being expected to respond to specific questions (Clarkson, 2008). Diaries can be used to collect both detailed information which provides in-depth insights into participants' feelings and reactions to specific incidents as well as standardized information such as the frequency with which particular work tasks are undertaken and their duration. Whilst diaries allow the collection of data over time in, at least for the researcher, a relatively less intrusive and less labour-intensive manner than procedures such as interviews and observation, the data obtained is dependent upon the participant actually completing their diary. This is particularly problematic over longer time periods where participants often withdraw due to the level of commitment required.

The utility of *participant diaries* depends upon participants' willingness to complete the diary. This is particularly important, as it is often difficult to find participants who are willing to keep a diary due to the effort involved. Consequently, it is worth selecting and subsequently briefing participants carefully and expecting that at least some will drop out as the research progresses. For unstructured diaries, typically participants will be asked to self-complete a series of entries over a particular period, and given a specified focus by the researcher. This can be the participants' ideas, reflections, thoughts, emotions, actions, reactions, conversations and so on. However, this request should be phrased in a neutral manner to try to standardize participants' entries. Participants will need to be directed regarding when and how to record their feelings in relation to the specified focus, but the content of the diary within these parameters will be decided by each participant. Alternatively, participants may be asked to self-complete a more structured diary. For these the structure can take a variety of forms ranging from prescribing some questions or areas for response, to asking participants to answer the same series of questions regularly over a prescribed period. Such structured diaries can appear very similar to questionnaires in their format and, once again, it is important to avoid leading participants to minimize bias in the answers. Prior to completing the diaries, participants will need to be briefed (see Box 3.2). The diaries, like observation records need to be completed as close as possible to the event. They can be written, audio recorded or, alternatively a video diary (Thomas, 2016).

Box 3.2   Aspects to consider when briefing participants about keeping diaries

- Brief explanation of the research referring to the information sheet:
  - o   purpose of research
  - o   effort involved in keeping a diary (what they will be expected to do)
  - o   how diaries will be used.
- Assurance of rights to anonymity and/or confidentiality.
- Request for consent.
- Detailed written explanation of how to complete diaries:
  - o   how to make entries
  - o   when to make entries
  - o   focus of entries
  - o   contact details (name, email address, telephone number) for queries.
- Detailed written explanation regarding returning of materials:
  - o   what materials to return
  - o   how to return materials
  - o   when to return materials
  - o   to whom to return materials.

Questionnaires, despite rarely being discussed in relation to case studies, offer a useful tool for collecting structured data that can be easily quantified by asking precisely the same set of questions to a large number of respondents. Whilst this procedure is not used frequently, as it does not offer in-depth insights, it can provide useful contextual and comparative numerical data for both multiple and embedded case designs. If questionnaires are used where there is a complete list of potential respondents, they can provide a means of collecting data from a probability sample and statistical generalizations made. Although rarely incorporated in case studies, the main use of questionnaires and the data they collect is in combination with other data sources. In such situations, respondents are unlikely to be selected using probability sampling. This does not however remove the need to pilot test the questionnaire to ensure, amongst other things, that the questions are collecting the required data.

Finally, in this discussion of the 'collect data' component, it is worth noting that writers on case studies differ in their views on the role of a *pilot study* in preparing for the study. Some like Yin (2014) argue that for pilot or preliminary case studies to develop, test and refine the procedures that will be used in the formal case study. Whilst these may be argued to be possible within an orthodox approach, we believe you need to be a bit more circumspect regarding pilot testing your data collection procedures, particularly when using data collection tools other than questionnaires. As we have already noted, every case is different and, as a consequence, the data sources that were not available in one case or collection procedures that did not work as well as expected may be available or work well in another case. In addition, we consider that not using data collected from a pilot case study is both wasteful of potentially useful data and could be considered unethical. Despite this, and as Stake (1995) notes, trying out interview questions in pilot form, at least with a knowledge-able friend or in mental form, should be undertaken. This can also help improve your interviewing skills.

ANALYSE DATA, WRITE AND REPORT FINDINGS

Although the focus of this book is the preparation for collection and subsequent col-lection of data when undertaking case studies, it is worth noting that how the data will be analysed needs to be considered prior to data collection. This is particularly important given the potential breadth of analyses you could undertake. The pro-cedures chosen to collect data will largely determine the form of the information collected and the potential analytic techniques that may be used. You need to be certain that you either have, or can develop the necessary expertise to undertake these analyses. In addition, you will need to think about how you will weave the different forms of evidence together to construct your case study to answer your research question and provide clear insights. These will need to be linked back to the nature of theorization you intend to undertake and whether you are looking to develop your explanation at the individual or institutional level when answering your research question.

Invariably your case study research will be written up as a dissertation or project report for your university. However, if you have promised an organization that, in return for providing access, you will give them a summary of the findings, you also need to ensure that you allow time for this. Remember a report for an organization is usually quite different in form to the academic dissertation required by a university.

SUMMARY

This chapter has provided an overview of the tasks that need to be completed as part of a case study strategy, focussing upon the components up to and including data collection. We have considered differences between research questions associated with orthodox and emergent case study approaches and the role of literature in developing these questions. We have then looked at designing the study and the link between different approaches to theorization, the research question and units for which analysis will be undertaken. We have identified those aspects that need to be considered when preparing to undertake a case study and highlighted differences between an orthodox and an emergent approach prior to the main ways of collecting data to provide evidence. Although not the focus of this book we have highlighted, albeit briefly, where aspects of the components considered are most likely to impact upon the 'analyse data' and 'write up and report findings' components.

4

CONDUCTING CASE STUDIES

INTRODUCTION

This chapter builds on Chapter 3 providing insights regarding how the basic components of case study can be combined to conduct research. In earlier chapters in this book we discussed how case studies are particularly useful in answering how and why questions, where the understandings and explanations sought require in-depth investigations of a real-life setting. We also introduced two distinct approaches to case studies in business and management: the orthodox and the emergent, revealing that the basic components that make up case study research can be combined in markedly differing ways (Chapter 3).

Recognizing that your research will be time constrained, within this chapter we consider how to operationalize the basic components of case studies to collect data. As such we are concerned with the practicalities of defining the research question, reviewing literature, preparing for study and collecting data, and exploring how these coalesce in the conduct of firstly orthodox and secondly emergent case studies. Despite our focus in this book on data collection we do where necessary refer to analysing data as, particularly in emergent case studies, this is an integral precursor to the 'prepare for further study and collect more data' component.

This chapter comprise two main parts. Part 1 focusses on practicalities of conducting orthodox case studies and Part 2 on the practicalities of conducting emergent case studies. Each part commences with a relatively detailed 'box' offering an illustrative example of either an orthodox (Part 1) or an emergent (Part 2) case study. Subsequent discussion within each part refers to the associated illustrative example when exploring how the case study approach in question might be operationalized.

In Part 1 this discussion follows the linear approach of an orthodox case study, discussing each of the components in turn, thereby reflecting the process illustrated in Figure 1.1. Having outlined the operationalizing of individual components, discussion in Part 2 follows the temporal flow of the boxed example, highlighting how components are interwoven and need to be re-visited within the fluid nature of an emergent case study. In doing this, we hope you will be able to compare and contrast orthodox and emergent case studies more easily, recognize the differences between the two approaches and their use of the component parts and apply this when conducting your own case study research. We therefore recommend that you read both parts of this chapter in the order they are presented, and ensure you are fully familiar with the boxed examples and each of the components as discussed in Part 1, before proceeding to Part 2.

PART 1: CONDUCTING ORTHODOX CASE STUDIES

Introduction

Orthodox case studies are often portrayed, explained and discussed in a linear manner. While this is a simplification and there will be some overlap between components, the conduct of an orthodox case study is essentially undertaken in sequence. Following the illustrative example (see Box 4.1), we first discuss how to 'review literature' and 'define research questions'. Next we consider how to 'design [the] study.' This is followed by advice on how to 'prepare for study and collect data'. Within this component we focus on the use of secondary data, and the operationalization of semi-structured interviews, participant and unstructured observation and participant diaries.

Box 4.1   An orthodox case study[1]

Jem was interested in why people trusted and distrusted each other. She was particularly excited by how this impacted on those working in organizations. In one of her course lectures, she had been introduced to alternative theoretical models of trust and distrust; her lecturer referring to a review article by Guo et al. (2017). These theoretical models summarized three distinct views within the academic literature:

1   Trust and distrust are opposites and an absence of trust is the equivalent to distrust.
2   Trust and distrust are opposites but an absence of trust does not necessarily mean distrust, it is possible to be ambivalent.
3   Trust and distrust are separate dimensions rather than opposites, so it is possible to be both trusting and distrustful at the same time.

Jem wondered whether employees were trusting, distrustful, trusting and distrustful or neither trusting nor distrustful of each other and why this happened. She phrased this as an initial research question:

- Are employees trusting, distrustful, both trusting and distrustful, or ambivalent of other employees in their organization and why is this?

However, she needed to find out more about what was already known about trust and distrust. Her initial search of the databases Business Source Premier (EBSCO) and Emerald Insight using the search terms 'trust' and 'distrust' revealed over 60 articles with both trust and distrust in their titles. Many of these had been referenced in the Guo et al. (2017) article. She decided to download and read those that looked most relevant. A number had collected empirical data using case studies. One of these, Saunders et al. (2014), had highlighted the importance of understanding fully the precise focus (the referent) of trust or distrust; in other words, whom or what was being trusted or distrusted and in what context. This article had used two different organizations, collecting data from individual employees to better understand trust and distrust judgements. The research reported revealed that individual employees were rarely both trusting and distrustful of other individual employees or their organization, being either trusting, distrustful or ambivalent. It also revealed that trust and distrust were separate dimensions, which manifest themselves in different behaviours and emotions. This article concluded: 'To improve our understanding, these differences in trust and distrust constructs, and the associated experiences, need to be explored across a broad range of organizational contexts and levels' (Saunders et al., 2014: 662).

Jem wondered if, as suggested, further research had been undertaken to improve understanding of the dimensions of trust and distrust in other contexts such as between individual team members. She noted down her thoughts as a question:

- Are trust and distrust separate dimensions rather than opposites, and do they manifest themselves in different ways?

She searched the databases for research articles about trust and distrust in teams, but found most articles only considered trust, referring to team members' decisions as trust judgements. She also noted that articles usually considered trust within one of a range of different team types, for example traditional work teams, limited life project teams or virtual teams. This she thought emphasized

(Continued)

the importance of context. Drawing upon these additional insights from the literature, Jem amended her research question to one she wished to examine in the context of work teams:

- How do trust, distrust and ambivalence manifest themselves?

Jem's study design needed to meet the assessment requirements of her degree programme. She needed to collect her own data (rather than use secondary data), undertake her research complying with the university's ethical policy and submit her dissertation no later than the specified deadline.

Jem decided, partially for the sake of convenience, to select a company local to her university to use as a single case study. She examined a local online trade directory to identify companies likely to have employees working in project teams and then used the search engine Google to gather more secondary data about each of them. From this she developed a shortlist of possible companies from which she could select a confirming or disconfirming case.

Jem also used the literature to theorize the type of data she would require from a case study company. She already had basic data about each potential company such as number of employees and location and copies of the previous annual reports from her online searches. However, she needed to collect data from employees about instances where they had felt trusting, distrusting or ambivalent about other employees in their team and how this was manifest in terms of their behaviours and emotions. These data would be analysed at the level of the case and used to confirm whether the differences in trust and distrust constructs, and the associated experiences suggested in the literature, did occur in a different organizational context. She would be seeing whether the theory applied in a new context. She considered that data to see if this could be collected by conducting semi-structured interviews with individual team members. She telephoned the first company on her list and explained that she would like to interview a sample of employees about how they felt when working in teams and how this would allow her to understand the trust and distrust judgements made. Eventually the fourth company she contacted agreed to discuss her research with her. After a face-to-face meeting and an exchange of emails, Jem received an email stating this company were willing to allow her to interview up to 10 employees.

Jem developed a research proposal and submitted it to her supervisor. He asked her to develop it further as a case study protocol focussing in particular on how she was going to collect the data to answer her research question and issues of ethics. She devised an interview checklist, which she included in her protocol.

After discussion with her supervisor and pilot testing, Jem finalized her interview checklist. Following a brief explanation of her research and requesting the participant's consent, her opening question and associated prompt questions would be:

> Think of an event in the past when you felt especially trusting* of another member of your team. The person can be a supervisor, subordinate, or a colleague and you should not name them. Please tell me about the event.

> Probes:

- What happened?
- Was that person involved a colleague, supervisor or subordinate?
- What makes this event particularly significant?
- Could you tell me why you felt the way you did?
- Before this event, how did you feel towards that person?
- How did you act with that person after the event?
- Does your especially trusting* feeling towards this person still remain? If not, what happened to change that?

*These questions were repeated, replacing the phrase 'especially trusting' with 'especially distrustful' and then 'neither trusting nor distrustful'.

Jem undertook her interviews using this checklist and, where participants gave permission, audio recorded the responses. After the first five interviews, she began to see a pattern in their responses.

[1]Developed with support from Nevena Isaeva

Review literature and define research questions

Orthodox case studies begin with a relatively clearly defined research question, which is developed and defined from outside the case. For the vast majority of students, the process of defining the research question takes place alongside the review of the literature. In other words, the defining of the question is etic, being grounded in academic literature. We have already seen (Table 3.1) and discussed an example of an orthodox case study research question in Chapter 3. However, whilst there is considerable advice in research methods texts on formulating and clarifying research ideas using a variety of both rational and creative thinking techniques, there is relatively little about how to develop and refine an idea into a clear question when reviewing the academic literature.

Within orthodox case studies the process of reviewing the literature provides the starting point upon which you build your research. As you begin to read articles you will begin to think and make notes in your research diary about how they relate to your research topic. In doing this you will be starting to critique and synthesize relevant literature. This will provide a clear context for, and argument to justify why, your research question or questions are worthy of answering. You therefore need to ensure you have read and understand the key academic theories and research findings that are pertinent or that contextualize your research question and be up-to-date. You will need to make reasoned judgements about the value of the research you review (rather than just noting the findings) showing how this relates to your own using valid evidence in a logical manner.

Your lecturers and research methods text books will have probably emphasized the need to be critical when reviewing the literature. Critical refers to the judgement you exercise. It means that you need to make reasoned (justified) judgements about what you read and, after reading it, decide whether to include it in your written review. You also need to be able to juxtapose different viewpoints and using argument come to your own reasoned position. Sometimes this may involve you in criticizing conventional wisdom, or the dominant view, as well as recognizing that the research you are reviewing is not value free (Mingers, 2000). Undertaking (and writing) your critical review therefore means justifying your viewpoint with reference to literature and clear argument rather than just stating your own opinion.

We assume you will have already received advice on formulating and clarifying research topics and already have a research idea. We also assume that, like the student in Box 4.1, you have used lecture notes and text books to gain an overview of your research area and the key authors; and know how to generate search terms and search using full text online business and management databases such as Business Source Premier and Emerald Insight, as well as online specialized search engines such as Google Scholar. However, on their own, these will not help you to define the substance of your research question and contextualize and justify it in relation to what is already known.

Reviewing literature and defining and refining research questions is an iterative process of working up your initial idea and narrowing down the focus of your case study research to a specific question or series of two or three questions from your initial idea (see Box 4.1). In reviewing the literature, you are - for an orthodox case study - developing your understanding and knowledge of what is known about your topic and using this understanding to clarify, contextualize and justify why your precise research question or questions are worth answering. Undertaking a review involves you in establishing and writing about what research has already been undertaken, the associated findings and the theory or theories, and undertaking a constructively critical analysis of them (Wallace and Wray, 2016). Although it is unlikely to be possible to read everything on your topic, you should expect to read widely and also to be clear that an orthodox case study is the most appropriate approach for answering your research questions. Within your writing you therefore need to show that you have assessed what work is significant to your research and on the basis of this decided whether it should be included. This will necessitate you in becoming clear about the precise focus of your research, in other words in ensuring your research question is clear and being able to justify why it is worth answering. This process invariably takes time and as you work up your ideas, it is likely that your focus will become more precise.

If during your reading you discover the concepts, theories or research findings related to your research idea that are unclear, biased or inconsistent with other work these may help you begin to define or refine your research question. Business and management research, as reported in published articles, is predominantly based on spotting gaps in theoretical perspectives and filling these gaps (Alvesson and Sandberg, 2011). It is likely that for a Masters dissertation using an orthodox case study, your research will adopt this approach of gap spotting. Aspects where there is a lack of clarity, bias or alternatives such as the different theoretical opinions about trust in Box 4.1 suggest gaps in understanding, offering avenues for research. Your written review of the literature needs to highlight the gap and, using the literature you have reviewed, explain why it needs to be filled. By doing this you provide a clear justified argument for your own case study research. Occasionally, an article you review will actually highlight inconsistencies in the literature such as alternative theories, offering at least further partial justification for your own research question.

In Box 4.1, the student was already aware of alternative theories of trust and distrust. Initial reading of a review article, originally suggested as further reading for one of her classes, provided further insights regarding the competing theories and allowed the development of a research idea into an initial research question about the phenomena of trust, distrust and ambivalence. Although the question was to be answered using the context of work teams, the focus was on developing understanding at the phenomenon level. The initial review of the literature enabled the student to develop an understanding of competing theories, and emphasized the importance of context. One article's conclusion supported her belief that more research was needed to understand the phenomenon across different contexts, indicating that a case study could be used to develop explanations at this level.

The student's review of the literature highlighted that, compared with trust, there was a comparative lack of research on distrust; in other words, a gap in the literature (see Box 4.1). It also revealed that where existing studies adopted a case study design, this was often holistic, the single case being used to look at the phenomenon within a context where it was manifest. On the basis of further reading she was able to refine her initial research question developing three detailed questions that allowed her to understand how the phenomena (trust, distrust and ambivalence) were manifest in a new context (the specific type of team). Explanation from data collected to answer these questions would need to focus on the phenomenon level as she would be looking to theorize through analytic generalization.

We noted that in Box 4.1 the student had, through her review, established a gap in the literature, in this instance a lack of knowledge about a particular context. Gaps in knowledge can reveal potential research questions, which may be appropriate to case study research. In undertaking your critical review, and in particular through the process of drafting and redrafting your review you develop a clear argument about what is known and not known about your specific research topic. This provides the context and a reasoned justification as to why your research questions are worth answering.

When undertaking your critical review, you may surmise that, whilst the concepts, theories and research findings appear consistent, the empirical findings on which they are based are derived from a particular context and so may not be universal. For example, many widely cited concepts in business and management have been developed in Europe and North America (the West) and may, in some cases, not be fully applicable or require revision for non-Western contexts. In such situations case studies can be used to seek insights regarding how an existing concept or theory may be applied in a new context. Consequently, your research could consider the phenomenon represented in the theory or concept in the new context. Your research question would ask how that existing theory or concept applies to the new context. In answering this question, you would be developing an existing theory through analytic generalization.

During your Masters programme, you will have read a number of refereed journal articles reporting empirical research and become familiar with the usual structure of introduction, literature review, method, findings, discussion and conclusion. Where a journal article relates closely to your research, the literature review can be particularly helpful in indicating further articles and books that are likely to be highly relevant. These articles can also be of help in developing your research ideas and defining your research question. As illustrated in Box 4.1, many articles provide recommendations for further research, usually in their discussion or conclusions sections, that may provide a partial justification for your own research.

Review articles in refereed journals are likely to be of particular use in developing your research ideas and defining your research question. Such articles offer a considered review of the state of knowledge (already reported in the literature) about a particular topic, rather than reporting new empirical research, and provide full references to the associated articles. Although review articles will be found as part of a normal literature search, other search techniques are also helpful. Browsing the tables of contents on web pages of recently published issues of business and management reviews journals such as the *International Journal of Management Reviews*, the *Academy of Management Review* and the *Journal of Accounting Literature* which publish literature review articles, is one way of finding such up-to-date potentially relevant articles. Alternatively, your dissertation supervisor may be able to suggest potentially relevant review articles. It is also worth browsing the 'early view' articles on the journal's web pages. These are online versions of articles which have been published on the journal's website before inclusion in a specific issue of the journal. Those that are relevant can then usually be obtained using online databases such as Business Source Premier and Emerald Insight or searching on Google Scholar.

Review articles usually offer recommendations or outline opportunities for future research, these often also being phrased as questions for further research. Box 4.2 summarizes the opportunities for future research and two of the associated research questions outlined in a review journal article. These questions could be addressed using an orthodox case study. To answer the first question, you would need to design a study to establish how a particular phenomenon (change at the company head-quarters) had unfolded overtime. To answer the second question, you would need to design a study to establish how the processes of change (reported as 'initiation', 'deci-sion making' and 'implementation' in the question) functioned for this phenomenon. For these questions the focus is on changes at corporate headquarters and so the focus of interest is developing explanations that will support further conceptualiza-tion of this phenomenon. Theorizing will therefore be through analytic generalization.

Box 4.2   Using a research question from a review article

Kunisch et al.'s (2015) article 'Changes at corporate headquarters: Review, inte-gration and future research' in the *International Journal of Management Reviews* identifies five opportunities for future research to improve knowledge of:

1   The pressure for and resistance to changes at the CHQ (Corporate Headquarters),
2   Interrelationships among changes at CHQ,
3   Change processes at the CHQ,
4   Agents involved in changes at the CHQ, and
5   Adaptive and disruptive effects of changes at the CHQ. (Kunisch et al., 2015: 374)

In addition, the authors offer a series of 'exemplary questions' for the five oppor-tunities identified. These include, in relation to Opportunity 3, questions such as:

•   How do changes at the CHQ occur? In other words, how do they unfold over time?
•   How do specific processes of change at the CHQ, such as initiation, decision-making and implementation, function? (Kunisch et al., 2015: 375)

A common misconception is that reviewing the literature involves little more than creating an annotated bibliography of previous research articles and books you have read (Hart, 1998), rather than being critical. It is much easier to be critical if you think about the articles, books and book chapters you are reviewing in terms of themes they discuss, using your review to build up knowledge about those aspects or themes (and their authors). In doing this, it is useful to think of your review as a funnel in which you start at a more general level and then narrow down the focus to your specific research questions. You therefore need to read and make notes in sufficient detail to allow you to write a constructive critical analysis in relation to your research question using both theoretical and empirical research that supports and opposes your ideas. The process of constructing a critical analysis is elaborated in Figure 4.1.

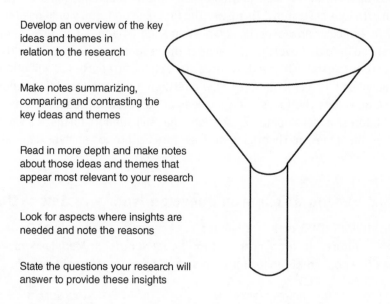

Develop an overview of the key ideas and themes in relation to the research

Make notes summarizing, comparing and contrasting the key ideas and themes

Read in more depth and make notes about those ideas and themes that appear most relevant to your research

Look for aspects where insights are needed and note the reasons

State the questions your research will answer to provide these insights

Figure 4.1 Constructing a critical analysis

Design study

For an orthodox case study, the research question or questions are usually fully formed before the study is designed and data are collected. This forms the base upon which you will design your research to be completed within the time frame prescribed by your Masters degree programme. In designing your study, you therefore need to:

1. Ensure the research question(s) is stated clearly and justified from the academic literature.

Despite having a clear research question when designing the study, it is worth noting that, as a case study progresses, the question may still be refined further in the light of data collected or further reading of the academic literature. Where this occurs, it is important that you note in your research diary the revised question(s) and the reasoning for the amendments along with any associated references to the literature.

It is also important to be clear about the precise focus of your theorizing from your case study as this will impact on the data you collect. This can be thought of as whether you wish to develop explanations from your case study that relate to a particular phenomenon (such as trust, distrust and ambivalence in Box 4.1), or are looking to provide explanations that relate to an institution such as an organization or particular context. This highlights the need to:

2. Clarify whether the research is looking to theorize about a phenomenon, an institution or at both levels.

Although data are collected from one organization, the research is looking to theorize, in other words develop explanations that relate to the phenomenon of trust/distrust/ambivalence, rather than to a specific institution such as the case study organization in which the phenomenon is manifest. This necessitates theoretically informed selection of cases and research participants.

We noted in Chapter 3 that case study designs, particularly those that are orthodox, are often presented using Yin's (2014) four-fold typology. The importance of this typology for orthodox case study design is its highlighting of the need to specify both the number of cases that will be included and how the data from the case or cases will be analysed, in particular to:

3. Specify whether data will be collected from a single case or multiple cases and give reasons why.
4. State whether the analysis will look at each case as a whole unit or divide each case into sub units and give reasons why.

In addressing these aspects, it is important to make a note in your research diary of the associated reasoning for the choices you make as these justifications will be reported in your dissertation. In Box 4.1 a single case is used to establish whether the phenomenon applies to a new context. This case has been selected as a confirming or disconfirming case – as discussed in Chapter 2 – and will be used to increase understanding of the phenomenon of trust/distrust/ambivalence. The case will be analysed holistically, in other words as a single unit, rather than dividing it into sub units. Data collected from employees about their understandings will be used to theorize through analytic generalization. This choice of a single holistic case can be justified, in part, by referring to other researchers who have used a similar method to build theory through generalization. The recommendation in the literature for further research in different organizational contexts provides additional justification.

Within orthodox cases, the data required invariably depends on the research question and the nature of theorization. Invariably there is a need to provide background information to place the case study within a broader context. Consequently, even if when gaining access you promise a case study organization anonymity, you will still need to offer sufficient detail to enable the context to be understood whilst ensuring that it cannot be identified. Contextual details usually provided include an approximate number of employees, the sector and the region or country within which the case study is located. You will also need to theorize which data are needed to answer the actual research question(s) and the likely sources from which that information may be obtained:

5. Establish the data required to answer the research question(s) enabling theorization at the proposed level and units of analysis and give reasons why.
6. Specify in overview the likely sources from which these data can be obtained and confirm feasibility of physical access.

Establishing the data required to answer the research question(s), as well as contextual data, is not the same as specifying (or confirming) from where or how the data will be obtained and that it will actually be feasible to collect it. In Box 4.1 the student wishes to collect data regarding how the phenomenon (trust, distrust or ambivalence) manifests itself. The literature reviewed provides some insights regarding the data required; in this box, data on individual employees' behaviours and emotions. Here as in other case studies, it is helpful to think about the level of detail in which these data are needed and how they related to theory and key concepts in the literature reviewed as this can provide a justification for the choices made.

In Box 4.1, the use of employees as a source of data was adopted from previous research; employees working in teams being specified by the researcher when requesting written permission for physical access to collect such data. It is advisable to obtain written permission confirming it will be possible to collect data. It is also worth noting that, in addition, informed consent will still be required from participants when collecting data. Whilst contextual data can often be gleaned from secondary sources – such as organizations' web pages, annual reports and, perhaps, the media – it is important to establish that these data are actually available in the proposed sources rather than just assuming they are.

Prepare for study and collect data

Invariably aspects of preparing for study and collecting data overlap with the design study component. As we noted earlier, it is helpful if physical access to the case study organization(s) is requested and hopefully confirmed during the design study component as this can prevent wasting time researching an organization, which subsequently declines to take part. Box 4.3 outlines a series of aspects to consider when requesting physical access.

Box 4.3 Aspects to consider when requesting physical access

- Allowing sufficient time.
- Making use of existing contacts as well as developing new contacts.
- Preparing a succinct account of the purpose of your research, the type of access required and the possible benefits.
- Ensuring familiarity with the organization or group before requesting access.
- Using suitable (non-academic) language.
- Offering a range of ways to reply (e.g. email, telephone, mail).
- Following up the initial request if there has been no response after a reasonable time.

In addition to obtaining physical access, it will be necessary to obtain cognitive access and informed consent from those who take part. Cognitive access refers to gaining individual participants' permission to be interviewed or observed within agreed limits. As part of this, universities' ethical procedures normally require researchers to provide each participant with an information sheet, explaining the purpose of the research project, what their participation will involve and how the data will be used. They also expect researchers to obtain each participant's formal consent using a signed consent form. Such forms are used to confirm explicitly that the participant has been informed about and understands the purpose of the research, has had the opportunity to seek clarification, that their participation is voluntary and that she or he agrees to take part. The form also allows each participant to signify agreement or otherwise to, for example, an interview being audio recorded. Although within case studies, questionnaires are less frequently used to collect data, it is worth noting that whilst some university ethics committees allow consent to participate to be implied or inferred simply by the returning of the questionnaire, others now expect questionnaire respondents to explicitly agree to take part as part of the questionnaire. As noted earlier, where you use organizational documents as secondary data, such as internal reports that are not available publicly, ensure that you have explicit permission to do so.

In Chapter 3 we offered an overview of a range of secondary data sources and primary data collection procedures used in case study research highlighting their advantages and disadvantages. Within orthodox (and emergent) case studies a variety of secondary and primary data sources are normally used together, the precise combination being dependent upon the research question. This use in combination reflects the first of Yin's (2014: 118) four principles of data collection: 'use multiple sources of evidence'. It emphasizes what Yin considers to be a major strength of case study data collection; namely drawing upon and using a variety of data sources the conclusion is likely to be more convincing and accurate. One reason for this is that, where multiple sources of data essentially suggest the same finding, this strengthens its validity. Different sources of data can be used to support different aspects of the research (Saunders et al., 2016). In Box 4.1 secondary data in the form of annual reports and organizational documents were used to understand the context within which data to answer the research questions were collected, this being undertaken primarily using semi-structured interviews.

Use of multiple sources of data creates a need for storage that allows it to be both easily accessible and meet your university's ethical requirements for storage of personal data. The need to organize and store all the data used in the case study is summarized by Yin's (2014: 123) second principle of data collection: 'create a case-study database.' This is separate from your dissertation and comprises an orderly collection of all the data you have collected including organizational documents, interview transcripts, field notes, your research diary and copies/notes of journal articles and books reviewed. Although much of these data will be stored electronically in word-processed files, the case study database is not necessarily computerized. Rather it is simply the organized archiving of all the data collected for the case study, so they can be more easily accessed.

Although orthodox case studies seek to define procedures in advance, these procedures cannot always be implemented as initially conceived. It is, thus, important to keep a research diary in which you document the changes to procedures and the forms of evidence collected to substitute for those originally conceived. Keeping a research diary is, in effect, ensuring that details about and reasons for the different forms of data are recorded to allow cross referencing between the data collection procedures, the data collected and their integration in answering the research question(s). This is summarized by Yin's (2014: 127) third principle of data collection: 'maintain a chain of evidence'.

Increasingly *secondary data* external to the organization are available online. However, it is important, as highlighted in Yin's (2014: 129) fourth principle of data collection, to 'exercise care when using data from electronic sources'. Whilst the number of online data sources continues to expand along with their ease of access, it is extremely easy to spend large amounts of time surfing the Internet. You therefore need to set limits as to the amount of time you will spend searching for potentially relevant secondary data online.

Searching for relevant secondary data, whether it is within or external to the organization, involves three interlinked stages:

- Establishing whether the data required are likely to be available;
- Locating the data;
- Assessing the suitability of the data.

There are a number of clues as to whether the secondary data required are likely to be available. Where journal articles refer to specific data that are relevant to the case study, these both provide an idea of the likely data available and, through the references, where to locate such data. Where references indicate data are stored in online databases or reports, it is usually relatively easy to locate the original source, either through your university library or online. References to unpublished surveys, company documents or archival records, although offering clues as to what secondary data might be available, are more difficult to find. However, they do indicate secondary data that might exist within a case study organization. To establish whether such datasets exist and whether you will be granted access to them, Saunders et al. (2016) recommend asking either the organization gatekeeper or the person responsible for information or data management. Online indexes, catalogues and government websites often contain direct links to downloadable quantitative datasets, often in spreadsheet format, that can provide contextual data. In addition, discussions with your dissertation supervisor or a librarian can often be helpful.

Once a possible dataset has been located, its suitability in terms of providing either contextual information for the case study or helping to answer the research questions needs to be assessed. Often the secondary data for which access is granted are not exactly what are needed. For example, data may have been collected a few years ago or relate to a broader range of organizations. Where this is the case an assessment needs to be made as to whether they are 'good enough'. This relates to the reliability and validity of the data, an assessment of which can sometimes be made by looking at the data source. Data from government sources are often perceived as reliable as are those from large organizations. However, it is also helpful to establish precisely how these data were collected, analysed and reported. Validity and reliability of within organization secondary data are often difficult to assess. Archival record data may be only partial or have been deliberately distorted to further a particular cause or the interests of a particular group. For written documents such as minutes, reports and emails, the intended target audience may reflect partisan interests. Therefore, as highlighted by Yin's (2014) first principle of data collection in orthodox case studies, we suggest triangulating the findings by using multiple, preferably independent, sources.

Chapter 3 also outlined a range of primary data collection procedures. Although you will almost certainly have had lectures on or read about semi-structured interviews, group interviews, participant observation, diary studies and questionnaires as ways of collecting such data, the lectures will not have focussed on their use within case study designs. It is not possible to discuss how you might use all research instruments, so we will concentrate on one method, *semi-structured interviews*, that are one of the most important sources of data in case studies and are often used in conjunction with secondary data and a permutation of other techniques. For orthodox case studies it is helpful to devise and, where possible, pilot test an interview checklist with one or two people who are similar to the intended participants. Even when this is not possible we would strongly recommend asking a friend to role-play an intended participant and interview them prior to your first interview. Box 4.4 provides a list of those aspects that are useful to include in your checklist and also offers an overall structure to the interview. However, it is worth highlighting that case study interviews do not always follow the order of topics on the interview checklist. Rather each topic is considered in the order that feels most natural for that particular interview.

Box 4.4   Aspects to include in an interview checklist

- Thank participant for agreeing to take part.
- Brief explanation of the research referring to the information sheet
  - purpose
  - themes that are likely to be covered
  - how the data provided will be used.
- Assurance of participant's rights to anonymity and/or confidentiality referring to the consent form.
- Request for participant's consent to take part (and to audio record the interview).
- For each topic to be covered (see Box 4.1)
  - potential opening question
  - potential probe questions.
- At the end of the interview thank participant for their time.

Participants interviewed should be chosen for their ability to provide the data required to answer the research question(s). This is not the same as selecting participants to give the answers that the researcher wishes to hear. Rather it is important to note in your research diary why particular participants were chosen, particularly if you have to interview people who hold positions other than those that you intended when you designed your case study. There are some authors (e.g. Creswell, 2007) who offer an estimate of the number of people that it is likely to be necessary to interview in a case study. However, even when conducting orthodox case studies, it should be remembered that case studies are not surveys, so it is not possible to generalize the number required by a formulaic prescription. The number will depend on several factors, most significantly the relationship between the research question and the people at the case study organization who have knowledge of the phenomenon being investigated. In Box 4.1 participants are chosen from one organization and only from those working in teams. Consequently, the ten participants may be an appropriate number.

In Box 4.4 we highlight the need to request participant consent for audio recording interviews. Whilst such recordings are extremely helpful they can only be used where the interviewer has been given permission. There is also a need to factor in sufficient time to transcribe or systematically listen to the interviews. Finally, audio recording an interview is not a substitute for taking notes. The audio recorder may fail to record, despite the record button being pressed! Furthermore, audio recordings do not capture settings and interactions where the evidence is primarily visual.

As the 'collect data' component proceeds, we recommend you reflect on the work undertaken to date in relation to your research question(s) using the following guide questions:

1. What is your research question(s)?
2. What do you now know?
3. What is your evidence for this?
4. Do you need additional data that has not been made available through interviews and what source is likely to provide that evidence?

Finally, once you are satisfied you have collected all the relevant evidence:

5. How does the knowledge derived from your evidence relate to the literature reviewed?

Undertaking this reflection and noting down your thoughts in your research diary will, we believe, help you in the 'write up and report findings' component (see Figure 1.1) of your orthodox case study approach.

Timeline week number → / Component activity ↓	1	2	3	4	5	6	7	8	9	10	11	12	13	14	15	16
Review literature and define research questions	▓	▓	▓											▓		
Design study				▓	*											
Prepare for study and collect data:																
– negotiate physical access						▓										
– gain ethical approval							▓									
– establish data sources								▓								
– collect data									▓	▓						
Analyse data											▓	▓	▓			
Write up and report findings					▓	▓					▓	▓	▓	£		$
Research diary entry	▓	▓	▓	▓	▓	▓	▓	▓	▓	▓	▓	▓	▓	▓	▓	

Figure 4.2 Gantt chart for an orthodox case study

* Deadline date for submission of draft literature review chapter
£ Deadline date for submission of complete draft
$ Deadline date for submission of dissertation

Managing your time

Within our introduction to this chapter we recognized that research would invariably be time constrained. Although deadline dates form part of the case study protocol (see Box 3.1) we believe it is important to also produce a schedule of the components of your research, the activities you plan to undertake within each, and how long they will take. By doing this you can help ensure that you will have sufficient time to complete your case study research and meet the deadlines set. Many students find it helpful to represent this as a Gantt chart (see Figure 4.2). This represents the time a component activity is likely to take by the length of its horizontal bar, and its start and finish times are represented by its position on the timeline. Deadline dates for submission are also noted on the chart.

Having considered orthodox case studies and the orthodox linear model, in Part 2 we consider conducting emergent case studies.

PART 2: CONDUCTING EMERGENT CASE STUDIES

Introduction

Within Chapter 1 we portrayed emergent case studies as evolving and becoming more clearly focussed as the research progressed. We also noted that the process invariably necessitated combining the components in different ways to an orthodox case study model as well as revisiting the components as the research progressed. This is important because although more fluid in its operationalization, an emergent case study will, as illustrated in Figure 1.2, still incorporate the components of 'define research question(s)', 'design study', 'review literature', 'collect data', 'analyse data', and 'write up and report findings'; the 'prepare for further study and collect more data' component emphasizing the iterative nature of this emergent process as the research progresses over time. For this reason, rather than discuss the operationalizing of each of the components separately, we focus on their interrelationships as the research develops. Alongside this we also highlight the importance of keeping a research diary throughout and, as part of this, noting as close to the actual time taken the decisions made and actions taken along with their justifications.

We begin our consideration of conducting emergent case studies with an illustrative example (see Box 4.5). Drawing on this example, we discuss how the components interrelate as the research develops. We begin by exploring the genesis and initial definition of research questions highlighting interrelationships, particularly with regard to the early 'design study' component, initial use of the 'review literature' component and preliminary engagement with the 'collect data' and 'analyse data' components. We then consider the interrelationships between components as the case study becomes increasingly clearly focussed and the research question more tightly defined. In particular, we discuss how these can operate in combination through a number of iterations of 'preparing for further study and collect more data', revisiting the 'review literature', 'collect data' and 'analyse data' stages to clarify the 'define research question(s)' and add precision to the 'design study' components. Finally, we return to the 'design study' component highlighting its emergent nature as the study progresses.

Box 4.5   An emergent case study

Depak had been wondering what to do for his dissertation. He was interested in small businesses and planned to start his own business after his degree. Depak's elder brother had started a small business six years previously importing Indian foodstuffs and spices and Depak wondered if his dissertation could be based on some aspect of his brother Madhuk's business. They agreed to meet to talk about possible ideas for the dissertation.

Prior to meeting with his brother Depak re-read his lecture notes on small and medium sized enterprises (SMEs) and summarized them in his research diary along with a few potentially useful references that the lecturers had suggested for further reading. He noted that in 2015 there were 5.4 million businesses in the UK employing less than 250 people, providing 15.6 million jobs and equating to approximately 60% of the private sector workforce, the vast majority, unlike his brother's business, having no employees (Department for Business Innovation and Skills, 2015). He was also reminded of the precarious nature of SME existence: the UK Office for National Statistics (2015) estimates indicate that fewer than 61.5% of SMEs were still trading three years after start-up, with fewer than 42% surviving after five years. He also used Google to search for his brother's business noting that, although the web page seemed somewhat out of date, there was some useful information that he recorded in his research diary.

During the conversation Madhuk talked about his plans for growing the business and employing more people. His existing customers were placing larger orders each time and a few potential new customers had approached him. Depak asked how potential customers heard about him and was told it was almost entirely by recommendations from existing customers. Madhuk highlighted that growth was dependent upon obtaining additional finance. He recalled how, when starting the business, he had borrowed money from relatives, but now he needed a larger amount. He had applied to the major high street banks for a loan, all of who had refused him, although he was not clear why. Madhuk wondered if Depak could provide insights regarding where he might be going wrong using it as a case study for his dissertation. Depak noted briefly the issues that they had discussed in his research diary as potential research questions:

(Continued)

- How does an SME win new business?
- How does an SME obtain finance?

Over the next week, Depak began to review the academic literature on SMEs. He started by reviewing the literature on SME growth and finance. This revealed that, like Madhuk's business, SMEs grew their business through word of mouth advertising, investing time in building up a network of contacts, referred to in the literature as social capital (Schoonjans et al., 2013). He also noticed that research had reported an increase in the use of online networking by SMEs (Harris et al., 2012). Journal articles on SME finance revealed that many SMEs used a range of sources to finance their start-up. The most important was, like Madhuk's business, loans from families and friends (Gray et al., 2012), although banks were the most widely used source of 'external' finance (Department of Business Innovation and Skills, 2012). However, research (for example Vos et al., 2007) also suggested a puzzle as, unlike Madhuk's business, most SMEs who sought external funding subsequently appeared able to obtain the money they requested. His brother's company could provide an interesting case study of the issues facing an SME that wanted to grow, but he needed a clearer focus. The literature had suggested two possible foci – networking and finance. On the basis of this reading and of the research methods literature he considered that he could adopt a research design using his brother's small business as a case study. The initial part of his emergent design involved formally interviewing his brother to help decide which of two possible research questions he was going to pursue:

- How does [SME name] use different forms of networking to develop social capital to support growth?
- Why was [SME name] unable to obtain finance for growth subsequent to start-up?

In order to start exploring the potential of these two research questions, Depak thought about the early stages of his study. His university had said any dissertation that did not follow ethical procedures and ensure participant's informed consent would automatically fail! He would therefore need to interview his brother formally and obtain his consent to use both data already gathered, such as through earlier conversations, and any future data collected. For the interview Depak had prepared an information sheet and consent form and noted a number of areas based on his reading about which he wanted to ask his brother. Although Madhuk was willing to talk about his networks, it seemed to Depak that the main issue was not being able to borrow money to expand his business. His brother repeatedly stated how it was impossible to get banks to lend his SME money, and showed him the loan applications he had submitted to banks that year and their subsequent letters of refusal. Depak asked him to tell him about each of the applications, explaining the process from start to finish as fully as possible. He also asked for copies of the documents.

Listening again to the audio recording of the interview, it was clear to Depak that the issue of major concern to Madhuk was being unable to gain finance to expand his business. Depak decided to focus his review of the literature in this area and noted that authors (Department for Business Innovation and Skills, 2013; Gray et al., 2014) highlighted the issue of information asymmetry and in particular how SMEs were either unaware or unclear of both potential sources of finance, the lending criteria these sources used and how the criteria were applied in practice. Literature also highlighted a problem regarding financial literacy amongst some SME owners (Sian and Roberts, 2009). From the audio recording, it appeared that Madhuk was unaware of the criteria used, the importance of a business plan, and the need to provide security, such as the family home, for the loan. Depak wondered if this was actually the case so he decided to compare Madhuk's interview responses with his actual loan applications. The literature had also highlighted a number of other sources that SMEs could use to finance growth, none of which Madhuk had mentioned. He noted in his research diary that this could be either due to Madhuk not being aware of these sources, or because, as interviewer, he had not asked the question. He would need a further interview.

Analysis of the loan applications suggested Madhuk was not aware of the importance of the application process and, in particular the information provided. Madhuk appeared to have spent relatively little time filling in the online applications, often leaving questions unanswered, and his business plan – a requirement for all loan applications – had not been updated for two years. Depak noted a series of questions he wanted to ask about the application process, the support Madhuk might have received from business advisors and his accountant, and the nature of the contact he had with the banks during the application process. Depak also noted that he still needed to be clearer about the actual financial support that was potentially available. He felt the focus of his study was now clear and noted a question that, as well as being grounded in the literature, he felt would enable him to understand the case:

- How and why did [SME name] seek to finance growth and why was this not successful?

(Continued)

Depak prepared an initial plan for further study to address this question. He would undertake a further interview with Madhuk concentrating on each of the applications for funding and the support and advice he had received. He would analyse each actual application, including the business plan, in detail alongside the documentation provided by the lender. This would be set within a broader context derived from the literature regarding what was known about sources of finance available to SMEs for growth and reasons for securing and not securing it. Through this he believed he would also be able to offer his brother useful advice and submit a dissertation that met his university's assessment criteria by the deadline.

Genesis and initial definition of research questions

Unlike orthodox case studies, emergent case studies rarely begin with clearly defined research questions; rather these emerge from the case – helping to define the boundaries of the case – and evolve as the study progresses. Emergent research questions are often initiated through some form of an existing connection that a researcher has with the organization, group or sector in which the case study is located. For many students, particularly those in employment and studying part time, their case will emerge from working in an organization, the impetus for the research developing from an issue or problem observed in that organization. In Box 4.5, the initial impetus for the case study question was a variant of this; the researcher's interest in small businesses and knowledge of, and connection to, an existing small business founded and owned by his brother. Such existing connections are often important in obtaining physical access to a potential case study organization. For example, employed students' line managers often act as gatekeepers helping them negotiate access to undertake the research. Research questions that emerge from an organization or organizations with which the researcher is familiar become clearer as the research progresses, the focus often being upon a particular phenomenon and the institutional level of analysis.

Within the case study in Box 4.5 it is important to recognize that, despite the researcher not having a clear problem or question the research was going to address, he still prepared for his first meeting with the owner and gatekeeper, ensuring he had a basic overview knowledge of both the field and the potential case-study organization. This comprised a preliminary brief engagement with both the 'review literature' and 'collect data' stages. For this initial review of the literature the researcher used a combination of a few key academic journal articles and books recommended by a lecturer alongside lecture notes to re-familiarize himself at an overview level with SMEs and issues likely to be facing them. Drawing on this preliminary review of the literature he noted in his research diary aspects that could be of importance such as the precarious nature of SMEs' existence. Whilst reviewing the literature, he also used online secondary sources beginning to 'collect data' from multiple sources to familiarize himself with the potential case study organization, again documenting aspects he considered might be useful in his research diary. However, as illustrated in Box 4.5, in an emergent case study you are unlikely to be clear regarding the precise focus of the research. Consequently, you are likely to have to revisit both 'review literature' and the 'collect data' stages as your research becomes more focussed. For this reason, we consider it crucial to note both the aspect considered important and the full reference of the source (see Box 4.6) in your research diary along with any crucial web links. We also recommend, where possible, downloading copies of online reports and datasets and, as discussed earlier, storing them in an orderly manner in some form of case study database. As part of this we suggest you keep a note of the file names and key characteristics of the data in your research diary (see Box 4.6) to allow them to subsequently be found more easily.

Box 4.6   Research diary entry relating to secondary data in Box 4.5

ESTIMATES OF SME NUMBERS

UK Department for Business Innovation and Skills produce annual estimates of the UK Business population as both reports and Excel spreadsheets. These include overall numbers as well as split by size, sector, region and trends over time. Can be downloaded from https://www.gov.uk/government/collections/business-population-estimates. Figures are updated annually in October.

- Downloaded the most recent spreadsheet and saved as: bpe_2015_detailed_tables.xls
- Downloaded the most recent report and saved as: bpe_2015_statistical_release.pdf

Report also includes useful definitions of SMEs.
> *Key fact*: Number of SMEs increased by 1.9 million (56%) since 2000. Account for 99.9% of Business Population. 99.3% have 49 or less employees.

Reference

Department for Business Innovation and Skills (2015) *Business Population Estimates for the UK and Regions 2015*. London, Department of Business Innovation and Skills Available at: www.gov.uk/government/uploads/system/uploads/attachment_data/file/467443/bpe_2015_statistical_release.pdf (accessed 25 June 2016).

Unlike orthodox case studies, and as highlighted by Stake (1995), 'collect data' is likely to begin even before there is a commitment to undertake a specific case study. Initial impressions collected informally as the researcher first becomes acquainted with a potential case contribute to the overall pool of data. This continues throughout the meetings with potential case study organizations to establish physical access. Such initial impressions can help 'define research questions' and are likely to influence the design of the study.

As noted in relation to orthodox case studies, we believe it is helpful to plan each meeting to request physical access. However, whilst many of the aspects considered when requesting physical access for orthodox case studies listed in Box 4.1 are likely to be relevant, you will be less clear of the precise focus of your research. Rather, your meeting will be like an exploratory interview, being a purposeful conversation (Kahn and Cannell, 1957) to gain insights into the broad topic and potential issues that may lead to research questions. Stake (1995), whilst recognizing the importance of creating records of such meetings, argues that rather than audio record or write furiously, it is better to listen, take a few notes which capture the key ideas and ask for clarification. Crucially, he emphasizes the need for time immediately after a meeting, to note both the key points and add an interpretive commentary. In Box 4.5 we see how such discussion between the researcher and the gatekeeper reveals two problems relating to the small business's expansion: winning new business and obtaining finance for expansion. At the gatekeeper's suggestion, these were used to provide a basis to start to define emic research questions grounded in the case study to understand the particular case, which could both satisfy the university's assessment criteria and provide answers of utility to the organization.

The 'review literature' component involves using existing research to help define and refine the emergent research questions and, not surprisingly, the points made in relation to orthodox cases also apply. However, as illustrated in Box 4.5 (and Figure 1.2) even early in the process the 'define research questions' component will be influenced by data already collected and analysed and which in turn will impact upon the design of the study. Whilst this may appear to be very messy, the interaction between the 'define research questions', 'review literature', 'collect data' and 'analyse data' will help you develop your understanding of the problem and progressive focussing of the research question and the research design (Parlett and Hamilton, 1976). Although your research questions are unlikely to be fully defined early in the research, it is important to continue to 'review literature' to help clarify understandings and contextualize ideas. It is worth noting such thoughts in your research diary to ensure they are not forgotten (see Box 4.7). It is also important to recognize that there will be a need to return to the academic literature and undertake a further review as the research questions become more clearly defined. In Box 4.5, reviewing both academic journals and published reports enabled the refinement of the research to address two possible foci; networking and finance. The first of these had clear links to the literature already reviewed; the second, whilst grounded in the academic literature, presented a puzzle as the literature seemed to suggest those SMEs that wanted to obtain finance were usually able to do so. These formed the basis of a refined research question, although we note that sometimes research questions 'pop up along the way' (Stake, 1995: 33).

Box 4.7   Research diary entry relating to literature read and data already collected in Box 4.5

IMPORTANCE OF SOCIAL CAPITAL IN WINNING NEW BUSINESS

Schoonjans et al. (2013) found SMEs grew their business through word of mouth advertising and by building up networks of contacts. This is referred to as social capital. [Article saved as pdf].

NOTE: I think this is what I heard about the case study SME from its owner.

TO DO: Need to check this is the case and see how what I heard compares with the theory.

TO DO: Search for more literature on social capital and SMEs.

In operationalizing the 'collect data' component you will, as a researcher, be watching the organization and recording your impressions; in effect undertaking unstructured observation. You will also be asking people questions, and listening to their answers, in order to better understand. This raises an important ethical question regarding the need to gain consent to collect and use such data. Whilst it is relatively easy to establish whether a person is willing to consent to being interviewed, the issue of consent is less clear regarding the use of data such as your initial perceptions of an organization upon your first contact. A number of researchers (for example Hookway, 2008) note that if what you are researching is in the public domain, and therefore available to people as a whole, it may be acceptable not to seek permission to use such data. However, given the uncertainty, we recommend you consult your university's ethical policy and, if in doubt seek consent. As noted in Box 4.5, the penalties for not following ethical procedures are often severe. Ethical policies also apply to researchers undertaking research in their own organization. If you are doing so, it is crucial that you are clear to others in your organization about when you are adopting the role of researcher, rather than just being an employee (Saunders et al., 2016).

Developing focus

As more data are collected and analysed research questions become more clearly defined and focussed and the study design more detailed. The literature is revisited and reviewed further, and the study design begins to become formalized as preparations for further study and collecting more data are made.

In Box 4.5 we see how the data collection is becoming more formalized as the student has prepared a participant information sheet and consent form, as well as drawing upon the literature reviewed to better understand specific areas about which he wishes to ask questions. In interviewing the company owner, the researcher is collecting data from a participant who knows a lot about the uniqueness and complexity of the case and so can be considered a key informant. This participant can provide observations, albeit often already second-hand, that the researchers would not be able to see for themselves (Stake, 1995). Consequently, the choice to interview this person is made purposively as he is critical to understanding the case, rather than on the basis of a need to understand commonalities and differences (Saunders, 2012).

Semi-structured interviews, although using a checklist of topics, are flexible and allow the researcher to probe further and follow up ideas as the interview progresses. In Box 4.5, this means the researcher is able to recognize those aspects of the phenomenon the participant considers crucial – namely, the relationship between banks and small businesses – and amend the focus of questioning accordingly.

We mentioned earlier that, in some instances audio recording of interviews might be neither appropriate nor possible. In addition, it may adversely affect the relationship between the participant and the interviewer, inhibiting some responses. However, where permission is given, audio recording an interview creates a permanent record, freeing the researcher to focus on what is being said rather than on making notes. Subsequently it provides an opportunity to listen to the interview on a number of occasions to reflect on possible interpretations of what has been said and which interpretation makes most sense in the context of other knowledge.

A key feature of case studies, already highlighted in our consideration of conducting an orthodox case is the integration of data from multiple sources. These include unstructured observations – discussed in Chapter 3 above – as well as secondary data.

Invariably as an emergent case progresses and the research questions become further focussed, the utility of different potential data sources to support the renewed inquiry will become clearer. These are likely to include secondary data held by the organization as well as that available online. We have already noted the need to exercise care with online sources and discussed ways of assessing the suitability of secondary data earlier in this chapter. However, one of the key skills when conducting emergent case studies is the ability to recognize potentially useful secondary data. Stake (1995) considers that researchers need to have their minds organized and yet be open for the unexpected. He also notes that, quite often, documents can provide records of activities that a researcher could not observe directly. The loan applications and subsequent letters of refusal outlined in Box 4.5 provide an example of such data.

Continued analysis of data collected is invariably undertaken using insights gained from literature already reviewed and will also prompt further, albeit even more focussed, reviewing of the literature based on those issues that seem more pertinent.

In undertaking this review, as with an orthodox case study, you still need to be critical. You therefore still need to ensure you juxtapose different viewpoints and using argument come to a reasoned position. You also need to consider how the findings from your research up to that time relate to the literature reviewed and where the literature suggests further research is needed to improve your understanding of the case, noting this in your research diary (see Box 4.8).

Box 4.8   Research diary entry relating literature read, primary data and secondary data

POSSIBLE INFORMATION ASYMMETRY?

Department for Business Innovation and Skills (2013) research highlights that many SMEs are unaware of potential sources of finance. [Article saved as pdf]

Grey et al. (2014) found many SMEs were unaware of lending criteria applied by high street banks including importance of a good business plan. [Report saved as pdf]

This is referred to as information asymmetry.

Sian and Roberts (2009) highlight problem of financial literacy amongst some SMEs. [Article saved as pdf]

Audio recording of Interview 1 indicates [transcription saved as Interview1.docx]:

- SME owner is unaware of criteria used to assess loan applications.
- SME owner is unaware of importance of a business plan to loan applications.

NOTE: There are a number of other sources of finance highlighted in literature (above) that the SME owner did not mention. This could be due to lack of awareness or because I did not ask.

TO DO:

1   Compare interview content with loan applications made and criteria stated by banks submitted to.
2   Analyse reasons given in letter for refusal of loans.
3   Search for further literature on information asymmetry and business funding.
4   Arrange follow-up interview with further SME owner.

As the research progresses, further study is undertaken and more data collected and analysed allowing the case to be more fully understood and the research question answered. Issues that emerge are probed and relationships teased out through a variety of different sources of data to check possible interpretations. Consequently, the researcher's task is to put forward an interpretation of the data collected that aids understanding (Stake, 1995).

Within an emergent case study, 'design study' rather than being a discrete component emerges and becomes clearer and more fully formed as the study progresses. Unlike the orthodox approach, the initial 'collect data' and 'analyse data' components are used to help define the research question, this being initially little more than a nascent idea or organizational problem, rather than a detailed protocol regarding how to answer an already formed question. During the genesis and initial defining of research questions, literature will begin to be reviewed. For the majority of emergent cases the focus will be on understanding and contextualizing the case and potential problem through description (Stake, 1995), rather than spotting potential gaps in knowledge. Theorizing is therefore likely to focus on the particular, explanations being developed regarding the phenomenon within the particular institution, using either a single case or embedded cases.

As with the orthodox case study approach we consider it helpful as your data collection finally draws to a close to reflect on the work undertaken to date in relation to your research question(s) using the following guide questions:

1. What is your research question(s)?
2. What do you now know?
3. What is your evidence for this?
4. Do you need additional evidence that you have not yet obtained and is there a source that is likely to provide that evidence?

Finally, once you are satisfied you have collected all the relevant evidence:

5. How does the knowledge derived from your evidence relate to the literature reviewed?

Undertaking this reflection and noting down your thoughts in your research diary will, we believe, help you in the 'write up and report findings' component (see Figure 1.2) of your emergent case study approach.

Data analysed to answer the research question will be drawn from multiple sources, at least some of which will only become apparent as the research progresses. For others, previous research reported in the literature will often provide an indication of the data likely to be available and of use. Consequently, an emergent approach will often lack certainty, particularly in the earlier stages. Throughout this process we believe it is crucial to keep a research diary recording both potentially useful insights and decisions made and the reasons for them as the process unfolds. This forms part of your case study database comprising all the data you have collected including organizational documents, interview transcripts, field notes and notes/copies of the articles and books read.

Managing your time

Within our introduction to this chapter we recognized that research would invariably be time constrained and, in relation to orthodox case studies we recommended producing a schedule of the components of your research, the activities you plan to undertake within each, and how long they will take. For emergent case studies, the more fluid and iterative nature of the process invariably means there will be more overlaps across the component activities (see Figure 4.3). However, despite this complexity, we still believe it can be helpful forcing you to be clear about how much time you have available for each activity and recognize that prior to some activities such as 'collecting primary data using interviews', other activities such as 'negotiate physical

Timeline week number → Component activity ↓	1	2	3	4	5	6	7	8	9	10	11	12	13	14	15	16
Review literature and define research questions	▓	▓	▓	▓	▓	▓	▓	▓	▓	▓	▓	▓	▓	▓		
Design study					*	▓	▓	▓	▓	▓						
Prepare for study and collect data:																
– negotiate physical access			▓	▓												
– gain ethical approval[1]					▓	▓										
– establish data sources					▓	▓	▓									
– collect data					▓	▓	▓	▓	▓	▓	▓	▓				
Analyse data						▓	▓	▓	▓	▓	▓	▓	▓			
Write up and report findings				▓	▓	▓		▓	▓	▓	▓	▓	▓	£		$
Research diary entry	▓	▓	▓	▓	▓	▓	▓	▓	▓	▓	▓	▓	▓	▓		

Figure 4.3 Gantt chart for an emergent case study

[1] Ethical approval required before primary data are collected using interviews
* Deadline date for submission of draft literature review chapter
£ Deadline date for submission of complete draft
$ Deadline date for submission of dissertation

access' and 'gain ethical approval' will need to be completed. As before, it is also worth noting deadline dates for submission.

SUMMARY

This chapter has outlined the operationalization of both orthodox and emergent case study strategies focussing on the components up to and including data collection. Within this we first considered the orthodox approach, noting that although it is often portrayed as a linear process this is a simplification as there is overlap between components. As part of this consideration we offered advice on 'review the literature', 'define research questions', 'prepare for study' and 'collect data' components. We then looked at the emergent approach to case studies focussing upon how these were operationalized in combination over a number of iterations. For both forms of case study, we emphasized the utility of a research diary within which to record decisions made and actions taken along with their justifications. We also highlighted the importance of managing time carefully to ensure deadlines were met.

5

EXAMPLES OF ORTHODOX AND EMERGENT CASE STUDIES

INTRODUCTION

In this chapter we provide published examples of both an orthodox and emergent approach to case studies. We have chosen to focus on two particular studies, one which demonstrates an orthodox approach and the other which illustrates an emergent approach, so that we can show the different starting points and development of the projects in some detail. We have chosen these studies not because they may be considered exemplary - although they have been acknowledged as having some academic value by being published in peer-reviewed journals - but instead because we were each involved in the studies. Mark was involved in the orthodox approach and Bill in the emergent approach. Thus, we are able to elaborate on issues from those studies that are relevant to this book. In the remainder of the chapter, we will discuss the orthodox approach first and then the case that used the emergent approach.

AN EXAMPLE OF AN ORTHODOX APPROACH: THE STUDY OF TRUST AND DISTRUST

There are numerous articles that may be classified as using an orthodox approach to case studies. These include Hadjikakou et al.'s (2013) examination of the economic contribution of a tourist market using a case study of Cyprus; Hansen and Jacobsen's (2016) longitudinal study of how public sector management reforms influence strategic management processes using case studies of five Danish Schools;

and Plakoyiannaki et al.'s (2008) examination of the interface between employee orientation and the customer relationship management process using a case study of a leading UK automotive services firm. In this chapter, however, we use an investigation into trust and distrust at two organizations that was conducted by Mark and two of his colleagues (Saunders et al., 2014). In this section, the term 'we' is used to refer to Mark and his collaborators who were involved in that study.

Background to the case

The relationship between trust and distrust of people who work in organizations had been theorized in a range of different disciplinary contexts. These include industrial sociology and organizational psychology as well as organizational behaviour. There were, however, conflicting understandings both with regards to whether trust and distrust were mutually exclusive experiences and on whether they were separate constructs with different expressions and manifestations. The regularity of change in organizations suggested to us that the presence or absence of trust or distrust could affect employees' willingness to co-operate with change and their subsequent willingness to deliver the services or products provided by organizations, and so could provide a useful context in which to examine these conflicting understandings.

The orthodox approach

In defining the problem to investigate, the first thing that we sought to do was, drawing on literature including our earlier research, adopt a taxonomy of concepts that would enable us to investigate the issues of whether trust and distrust were mutually exclusive and whether they were based on different considerations. This offered a broad taxonomy of different combinations of trust and distrust which are shown in Table 5.1.

Table 5.1   Potential combinations of trust and distrust

	Low (absence of) distrust	High distrust
High trust	Trusting	Both trusting and distrusting
Low (absence of) trust	Neither trusting nor distrustful	Distrustful

Source: Developed from Lewicki et al. (1998)

If the concepts were mutually exclusive and based on identical judgements, expectations and experiences, the assumption is that people who were trusting of the organization or a particular individual in relation to the change would appear in the top left hand corner of the table where there is high trust and low distrust; 'high' meaning existence and 'low' meaning an absence. In contrast people who were distrusting of the organization would appear in the bottom right hand of the table where there was low trust and high distrust. If categories of trust and distrust were dichotomous, these would be the only two categories; if the categories were the polar opposites of a continuum organized around the same judgements, expectations and experiences, some people who felt neither trust nor distrust (low trust and low distrust) would fall in the bottom left box. If instead, feelings of trust and distrust are borne out of different sets of expectations, the different feelings could co-exist and appear in the top right box in the table. We also noted from our earlier research (Saunders and Thornhill, 2004) that such feelings, where they existed, would vary in strength.

With the problem defined, we could proceed to designing the study. To be able to test out the ideas, we had to find an organization where it might be anticipated that there would be a high degree of trust during the change period and another where we anticipated a high degree of distrust when change was taking place. However, if the boundaries to the problem were to be controlled, it was necessary to choose two similar types of organization. In the end, we chose two UK local government authorities, albeit covering variations in expanses of the country and scale of services. The one where we anticipated there might be the most evidence of trust between the organization and its employees had been awarded the UK Government Audit Commission's highest rating when it had evaluated the authority and this organization had been commended for its approach to change that had been achieved without the need for redundancies. The authority where we anticipated there might be the most evidence of distrust had, however, engaged in extensive restructuring and compulsory redundancies which had been seen by some as involving considerable employee resistance. We decided to select randomly a proportionate number of employees from each organization stratified by directorate and level as defined by the employees' job role to explore the issue of their trust and distrust in their organization in relation to the change process.

We wanted to collect a quantitative form of data to measure the extent of trust and/or distrust and a qualitative form of data to delve deeper into the feelings involved in trusting and distrust. For the collection of the quantitative data, we had 49 cards derived from the literature and organized into six categories of feelings in relation to change. These were trust and distrust, expressions of high trust, manifestations of high trust, expressions of high distrust, manifestations of high distrust and other emotions. We asked each of our participants to sort these cards according to the extent that they felt the word or phrase expressed on the card in relation to the change process in their organization. The card sort allowed data to be collected that recorded each employee's strength of feeling for each of the 49 cards using a four-category ordinal scale comprising 'do not feel' (coded 'low') to 'feel to some extent' (coded 'weak'), 'feel strongly' and 'feel most strongly' (both coded 'high'). The meaning of these quantitative data about feelings were clarified subsequently by interviewing each participant about their categorization of the cards within the context of the change at their organization, beginning with those felt most strongly. Each interview lasted approximately one hour.

In analysing these data from the 56 participants (28 from each case study organization), we created categorized profiles according to the responses to the card sort and the interview data. This enabled us to write up and report our findings in Saunders et al. (2014) that suggested only a minority of our research participants fitted into the categories that supported the thesis of trust and distrust occurring simultaneously with regard to a single trust subject. Trust and distrust were separate rather than symmetrical constructs with differing manifestations and expressions. This indicates that different organizational interventions are likely to be required to reduce employee distrust than to build employee trust.

AN EXAMPLE OF AN EMERGENT APPROACH: THE STUDY OF INDIVIDUAL LEARNING ACCOUNTS

There are a range of articles that report on how case studies were revised or ideas changed in the course of a case study. For example, Otley and Berry (1994) report on the different points when empirical data in cases were collected and theories were introduced; Llewellyn and Northcott (2007) discuss how a reviewer's insights when a paper was submitted to a journal led to a marked change in understanding of the evidence collected; and - from the sociology of science - Collins and Pinch (1982) provide an exemplary illustration of how perceptions changed during the conduct of research into the phenomenon of spoon-bending. However, this part of the discussion will focus on the study of Individual Learning Accounts (ILAs) by Lee (2010, 2012).

Background to the case

ILAs were a flagship policy of the UK Labour Government that came to power in 1997. ILAs were intended as a means by which all adults would be supported in their pursuit of lifelong learning to help pursue career and life aspirations. The government set a target for one million accounts to be operational by April 2002. There were celebrations when the target was reached almost a year ahead of time and the government made several promises to extend the scheme. Then there were serious allegations of potential fraud and theft involving the scheme and it was closed on 23 November 2001. A number of government enquiries were conducted into abandonment of ILAs, some of which blamed 'failure' of the scheme on weak financial controls that allowed widespread abuse and fraud totalling £97 million by large numbers of unscrupulous providers. The government promised to relaunch ILAs and some years later, they introduced a much more limited scheme targeted at certain groups. The official explanation of these events appeared to be that fraud had resulted in the abandonment of the scheme but after financial controls had been tightened up, the scheme could be re-introduced.

Bill was not convinced of the official explanation. He (Lee, 2010) was to argue subsequently that there was evidence that the scheme had been successful. However, it had been abandoned in part because of over-expenditure caused by a finite budget to fund 1 million accounts and the opening of 2.6 million which threatened to generate expenditure for which there was no budget. He identified the potential for over-expenditure in the conflation of political philosophies. On the one hand, there was the Labour Government's continuation with the policy of marketization of public services that had been introduced into the public sector by the preceding, neo-liberal Conservative Governments. On the other hand, there was the new Labour Government's own idea of communitarianism where society was a need so everyone should have the opportunity to participate which led to a universal entitlement to adult learning. This combination resulted in many new private learning providers coming into existence to cater for the widespread demand which the government had not anticipated properly. He (Lee, 2012) was to explain how the unproven claims of widespread fraud and abuse in different government reports were to be amplified through the media and constituted the rumours that could precipitate a moral panic about how the alleged perpetrators of fraud constituted a threat to society in a way that was disproportionate to the actual problem. He discusses the way in which the method of the case study emerged for these papers below. The use of the personal 'I' in this context relates to Bill.

The emergent research approach

I had been an industrial sociologist and conducted different studies of vocational learning and so I was very interested when the new Labour Government proposed the introduction of ILAs in 1997. At this time in my academic career, I was in the process of transitioning as an academic from my origins of industrial sociology into the field of accounting and in 1999, I took up my first permanent job in that discipline at Sheffield University which was a couple of hundred miles from my then permanent home in Bristol. I had friends and acquaintances in Bristol who were then working for Training and Enterprise Councils (TECs) that had been established as employer-led private companies by the previous Conservative Government. My friends advised me that their intelligence told them that the new Labour Government were planning to abolish the TECs and replace them with a more representative non-governmental body, but the new government were concerned about recovery of the reserves of £150 million from public money that the TECs had built up from being paid by the previous governments to provide training. My friends suggested to me that ILAs provided a good device to achieve this objective and to reduce any threat of a legal challenge because of the principle of a universal entitlement in the ILAs. Given that the budget for the entire scheme for the first million accounts was £202 million over the course of the term of the Parliament and allowed £150 for each account opened, an additional £50 for Information Technology courses and monies for payment to *Capita*, the body hired to administer the scheme, it was not clear where additional funding would come from if more than one million accounts were opened.

I asked my friends about the funding problem that I had identified and they did not know whether more money would be made available, or whether expenditure would be limited to the first one million accounts and so would breach the universal commitment. Although they did not give me a satisfactory answer, I did not give too much thought to the issue at that time; but the conversations had taken place and questions that I had about the scheme would remain dormant until an answer was apparent. I knew, however, that I wanted to conduct research into Individual Learning Accounts as they provided a means by which I could combine my previous knowledge of vocational learning with my employment in accounting. So I attended a conference of the Association of Learning Providers where I listened to a number of presentations that included discussions of ILAs and I spoke with a number of the learning providers about their provisions and the types of courses that they were providing to people who paid with ILAs. All the schemes appeared to be worthwhile in encouraging people who had not previously been involved in learning to acquire new skills and I collected a number of business cards in case I wanted to interview learning providers later. I also started collecting newspaper articles about ILAs. Most of those articles provided positive coverage, although a minority did report a small number of learning providers, including *TeesLC* (pseudonym), which were allegedly providing poor quality learning and/or misleading prospective learners about the qualifications that they would receive. The outcome of those allegations was for the government to introduce new controls on learning providers if they wanted to be involved in the scheme.

When I first started teaching in my new role, I used overhead transparencies and a projector to deliver my lectures, tools that I had previously used when I had held teaching roles as an industrial sociologist. However, technology was advancing and I needed to learn how to use PowerPoint to make my visual aids more attractive and easier to update. At the time, I was commuting between Bristol and Sheffield, travelling to Sheffield on the Monday morning and returning to Bristol on Thursday after I had completed my teaching. My teaching commitments and travel arrangements prevented me from seeking guidance on the capabilities of PowerPoint at my place of work. I had previously checked the terms of the ILA scheme and found that I was entitled to an individual learning account and I applied. In the summer of 2001, I joined a course at one provider that had set up a facility with a number of modern computers in a large rented office in a block in Bristol. I got into the habit of going along there every Friday throughout the autumn and the man employed in the office showed me how to compose slides in PowerPoint and to embellish them in various ways. During the Fridays that I visited, there were a number of people coming in to use the facility. If I had a query in the week, I would email the man who worked at the facility and he would answer. Sometimes, he would send me links and information that he thought I might find useful. Then in November 2001, he asked me whether I had any information about the decision that had been taken to withdraw the scheme. I did not and we chatted about his concerns about future employment. When I went to the facility on the 23 November 2001, I was told by a general receptionist in the office that the learning centre was not open on that day and she did not know when it would next be open; the man who had been managing the scheme had phoned the owners of the building and said that he would not be going in on that day and he was not sure when he would next be in. I tried to email him, but found the email address that I had for him no longer worked. I found out later that day that the ILA scheme had been closed with immediate effect because of an attempt at a serious fraud. This allegedly involved somebody trying to sell a computer disc with numerous ILA account numbers so that someone else could access the funds.

At this stage, I had a number of disparate pieces of information, based largely on experiential knowledge. I had spoken with a number of learning providers who appeared to be running valuable schemes, I had attended one which seemed to offer very good value for money and while a number of newspaper articles had also indicated people's positive experiences through ILAs, some newspaper reports suggested inappropriate practice by some learning providers which had resulted in the government introducing additional controls. The scheme had then been closed because of an alleged attempt at serious fraud. If reference is made to Figure 1.2, I had begun to 'collect data' even though I had yet to define a research question. However, a broad one suggested itself of why was the scheme closed? To start to address this, I organized the information that I had collected so that I understood how the scheme was supposed to work and I knew that I would seek to gather more information about how the scheme did actually work in practice. In this regard, I conducted some initial analysis of the data that I had gathered, in the knowledge that I would add to that.

Further evidence was to appear in a series of reports by different government agencies. The first report was that of the Education and Skills Select Committee (E&SSC, 2002). A systematic analysis of this report highlighted three things. Firstly, there were competing explanations of the reason for closure manifest in the evidence that was provided to the Education and Skills Select Committee. On the one hand, there was the emergence of the argument that was to be repeated by other official reports that the weak controls had allowed unscrupulous bodies to abuse and defraud the scheme. On the other hand, there was another view that any abuse was small when seen in the context of the scheme which had attracted many hard-to-reach adults back into learning and the vast majority of learners were satisfied with the learning that they had undertaken. The scheme's abandonment – like previous demand-led schemes – was due to the high demand that had led to over-expenditure. Secondly – and in support of the first of the competing explanations above – witnesses reported that the government department under whose auspices the scheme fell, were withholding payments in excess of £15 million from 239 learning providers around whom they had doubts. The violations of 80 of these providers had been so severe that they had been referred to the police for investigation and at that stage another 16 were also being considered for investigation by the police. Also, the police had already arrested 45 people, 13 of whom had been charged, 10 had accepted cautions and one had already been convicted. Yet what the E&SSC (2002: paragraph 100) found it necessary to comment was:

> The Committee is concerned that, although there has been a multiplicity of rumour about scams and frauds, there is very little hard evidence of the extent and amount of fraud actually committed against the ILA scheme.

Thirdly – and in support of the second of the competing explanations above – there were an extremely low percentage of ILA holders who had complained about the scheme but an analysis of the information provided in the report suggested that expenditure for the total number of accounts that had then been opened would have risen to around £516 million rather than the actual expenditure of £293 million that was reported at that stage, if the scheme had not been closed. At this point, the evidence gathered had provided two potential answers to the broad question of why the scheme had been closed, so the findings remained inconclusive.

Two other formal reports appeared, one by the National Audit Office (2002) and another by the Public Accounts Committee (PAC, 2003). Analysis of their contents promoted support for the explanation that the cause was due to poor controls and abuse by a large number of learning providers. For example, the PAC (2003: EV34) accepted as evidence claims that:

> there were estimated net irregular payments of £97 million on the ILA programme, of which … £67 million was fraud and serious irregularities. The other thirty million was where learning was provided but did not fully meet the programme rules.

PAC (2003: EV28) also accepted as evidence the following details about the number of people involved which included '152 registered providers' about which there were serious doubts, 100 of which were being investigated by the police while a further 400 providers were also being pursued for their part in the abuse. Given that many people could have been employed at any one provider, this inferred that the potential number involved in any wrongdoing could have been considerable. In relation to Figure 1.2 above, there was as an emergent 'Design of study' and a constant movement between the stages of 'Prepare for further study and collect more data' and 'Analyse data' as I sought to find a satisfactory answer.

I kept checking on the website of the government department that had been responsible for the scheme and in newspapers for details about convictions and I wrote to the government department without response to enquire into the investigations and any intended prosecutions. Over this period, I was conducting other research about another government-supported learning initiative which brought me into contact with people who had been involved in the ILA scheme in various ways; one of whom was a senior civil servant at the relevant government department. I asked this person about details of prosecutions. In my other research, I also interviewed someone else from another body who had been one of the representatives interviewed about ILAs by the Education and Skills Select Committee. I also asked him about the operation of the ILA scheme, why it might have been closed and his understanding of any abuse and fraud. A friend also facilitated an introduction to someone who had worked for *TeesLC*, had been arrested and was still under investigation by the police for any fraud that had been perpetrated by that organization. He explained the events that had led to the arrest of people involved in *TeesLC*. As events were to materialize, the police found no evidence that he and others associated with *TeesLC* had been involved in any fraudulent activity and all charges against them were dropped. However, the owner of *TeesLC* and his wife were found guilty of the charges brought against them and these are the last convictions to date of those associated with ILAs. I continued to gather evidence right up to those prosecutions towards the end of 2008. When I put together all of the evidence that I had gathered about police actions, it amounted to 26 people being convicted, seven others being cautioned – lower than the number claimed in official reports because the official reports did not contain information that some had refused to accept the cautions – and the total losses from the proven misdemeanours amounted to £10.5 million, a sum that was considerably less than the amount alleged in the official reports. The total evidence suggested that any abuse was small when seen in the context of the scheme, ILAs had attracted many hard-to-reach adults back into learning, most ILA account-holders were satisfied with the learning that they had undertaken and the scheme was abandoned because the demand had led to over-expenditure.

At this stage, it became necessary to refine and extend the research question to ask not simply why the scheme had been abandoned, but why had it been introduced with the tension between the principles of universal entitlement when the cost associated with such a project could not be controlled if the provision of learning was through demand from learners for provisions from unspecified numbers of learning providers who were likely to expand to meet whatever demand existed. The literature on ILAs was sparse, so it was necessary to look at other literatures including that on the neo-liberal political philosophy of the previous Conservative Government which expressed faith in markets and private provision of state-sponsored services and the communitarian philosophy of the new Labour Government that sought to extend rights – particularly those associated with learning – to everyone. This required a constant movement between reviewing the literature, (re)definition of research questions and analysis of data that appears in Figure 1.2 as the evidence was examined against the refined research question until an argument that explained the pattern of evidence could be constructed and the final stage of writing-up and reporting the findings was reached in Lee (2010).

The gathering of the evidence that indicated that although two of the formal reports – namely those by the National Audit Office (2002) and by the Public Accounts Committee (PAC, 2003) – had suggested that abuse was widespread, these claims had not been confirmed by the number of arrests or the proportion of the expenditure on ILAs lost to fraud. This prompted another research question; namely did the concerns about ILAs constitute a minor moral panic and what was the role of the formal reports of regulators in generating that moral panic. Thus, in reference to Figure 1.2, the analysis of data led to new research questions that resulted in a further review of the literature around the concept of a moral panic so that the evidence that had already been collected could be organized to see whether the interventions of the regulators promoted a pattern that complied with that found in a moral panic and once the pattern had been documented, the findings could be written up in Lee (2012).

DISCUSSION

The purpose of this chapter has been to use published research that illustrates orthodox and emergent approaches to case studies as depicted in Figures 1.1 and 1.2 in Chapter 1 above. The orthodox case reported above conformed wholly with that depicted in Figure 1.1. While the diagram in Figure 1.2 can accommodate the process in the emergent case, it is possible to provide a specific representation of the process in the emergent case above. This is shown in Figure 5.1.

The two cases illustrate that, contrary to the inferences that may be read from some texts, there is no one best way to conduct all case studies. The orthodox approach was both possible and suitable for the investigation into trust as there were longstanding competing explanations about concepts in the literature and an empirical investigation could help to resolve that academic dispute. Concepts of trust and distrust could be defined clearly in advance and two organizations where changes were taking place could be selected and the boundaries to the empirical study could be defined. Findings from the study could then be constructed into a partially generalized statement and suggestions for extending the boundaries could be made. By contrast, individual learning accounts were a new phenomenon, the literature about them was sparse and the investigation into the ILA scheme's demise was taking place at the same time as events such as government agencies' investigations into the failings of the scheme, court cases into potential fraud and newspaper coverage of the scheme. Thus, the boundaries to the phenomenon were fluid and evidence had to be collected before research questions were fully developed. The refinement of the research question could only take place in conjunction with a review of the literature

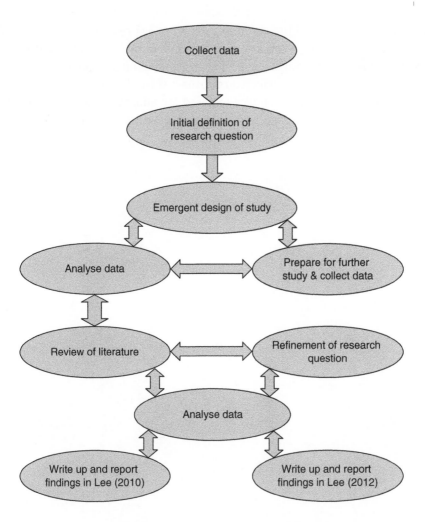

Figure 5.1 Specific process used in the emergent approach illustration

to identify the best way of explaining the pattern of the evidence that had been found. The novelty of the situation meant that theorization of the events had a strong degree of particularization although more widely applicable concepts were used in that explanation.

The cases reported here took place over a longer time period than is allowed for a dissertation. That is to be expected with published research. However, even if you are preparing a dissertation as your first ever piece of research, you may have conducted much of the necessary background reading for the dissertation beforehand as part of your taught programme. If you have previous experience, you may have already noticed issues of concern and started to formulate a research problem which you can refine by reference to the literature that you have read as part of your taught programme. Furthermore, there are large amounts of records kept nowadays – as in the form of the reports that were used in the emergent case approach above – so many case studies may be conducted retrospectively. While you may be unlikely to produce a dissertation to a standard required for publication in the time that you are allowed for the dissertation, it is possible to use either orthodox or emergent approaches when conducting your case study.

 **6**

CONCLUSIONS

INTRODUCTION

This book has presented two different approaches to case studies. Firstly, we have discussed orthodox cases that share many qualities with positivist approaches of defining the process in advance and conducting research in a linear and largely pre-defined way that tends to centralize propositional knowledge in the conduct of the case. We have also described emergent case studies that often draw on the use of prior experiential and tacit knowledge to realize the rich descriptions expected from case studies. While we have outlined two approaches, we are not advocating that they be seen as two sets of prescriptions. Our intention is for each to be read as a genre within which there may be different variations as is illustrated by the published emergent case cycling through a range of stages in a variety of directions in Chapter 5.

So far in this book, we have outlined the different approaches; considered the way in which each suggests it contributes to knowledge and the way in which research may be organized to realize that contribution; the tools that are used in case studies; the way in which those different tools are utilized; and we have reported on published examples of case study research. As indicated in Chapter 2, in any dissertation, there is an expectation that the author will conclude by reporting on the contribution that the dissertation has made and the provisos that they would put on their argument, many of which will be related - either directly or indirectly - to the method that has been used. Thus, in this final chapter of the book, we reflect, in turn, on the strengths and weaknesses of case studies which you may choose to consider when discussing the contribution of your own dissertation and its limitations. We will give most coverage to the limitations of case studies, not because we have no faith in the usefulness of case studies, but because we want you to be aware of the criticisms that are made of case studies and we want you to be prepared so that you can overcome those alleged limitations when conducting your case study.

THE BENEFITS OF CASE STUDY RESEARCH

However commonplace events may seem to the casual observer, all phenomena involving human beings have their unique qualities. One benefit of a case study is that it allows that particular event to be studied in detail so that its unique qualities may be identified. This is particularly important because most human phenomena are nuanced and dynamic and often need to be studied in the context of a longer sequence for their qualities to be drawn out. Case studies allow for such complexity to be researched and the necessary holistic vantage point to be adopted. Such advantages are enhanced when the phenomenon being studied is considered to be rare and unusual. Possible reasons why the phenomenon occurred can then be considered and the particular events that contributed to the manifestation of the case may be theorized to extend constructs and understanding. If this is the purpose of your research and your contribution to theory is to explain a rare and unusual event through particularization, it is important that you state this in your dissertation.

Another advantage of case studies is, as we have seen above, that some dimensions of findings can be generalized by stating the extent to which they are transferable to other instances and institutions. In Chapter 2, we provided details of a number of ways in which this might be achieved. As particularization and generalization are not mutually exclusive in cases, case studies enjoy a clear advantage over some other research approaches. However, we cannot emphasize enough that it is important to state clearly in your dissertation what part of your argument only applies to your particular case, what parts may be generalized, the limits to any generalization and why you believe that particular issues are only applicable to your case and why others may be generalized.

The conduct of case studies brings other advantages. As indicated above, emergent cases allow you to utilize your existing experiential and tacit knowledge to help identify problems, generate research questions, inform further data collection and guide your reading. Perhaps more significantly, such knowledge can also help you to empathize with the participants in your research and to understand and respect their interests and help them to realize benefits from your project. In this regard, case studies are also extremely useful in helping the expression of the voices of people whose interests are often ignored, but who may be affected by a particular change, institution or phenomenon and who merit having their voice heard. More generally, the desire to understand the same phenomenon from different people's viewpoints or from different theoretical perspectives in all types of case study means that data are gathered and used from a variety of sources. This creates a degree of flexibility as, if a particular form of evidence does not answer a question sufficiently well, the researcher may seek evidence from another source. Significantly, both quantitative data that provides some form of measurement and qualitative evidence that provides understanding of a process may be combined in imaginative ways to help explain a phenomenon.

WEAKNESSES OF A CASE STUDY AND WAYS OF OVERCOMING THEM

There is a downside to looking in depth at a particular phenomenon and that is a lot of data is generated in the course of a case study. Moreover, the information is often of varying types and so often requires analysing separately according to type. This would not be problematic if there was an infinite amount of time to analyse the data. However, all projects are limited by time and this constraint is even more acute in the course of a Masters dissertation when the whole project may have to be completed in a very short period. Two ways in which this difficulty may be overcome are: firstly, by dedicating most time to the analysis of the most important source and recognizing that the time that may be given to analysis of the other evidence will be limited; and secondly, by not waiting until all the data has been collected before starting to analyse particular types of data. For example, it may be that the case that you are studying is your own organization, or an organization where you have worked previously and will involve observations, analysis of documents and interviews. Once you have got ethical permission for your research, it may be that you use your existing knowledge based on prior experience and observations to write up what you understand about, for example, the context of what you are researching before asking one of the research participants to confirm your understanding. By writing up details of the context you have already completed part of the analysis. Similarly, you may collect documents on your first visit to the case organization. It might be that you intend to use the documents to describe a procedure. You can extract the information relevant to that procedure from the documents so writing up that procedure is the start of your analysis. An additional benefit of conducting analysis as you proceed is that you can use some insights from that analysis to enhance subsequent data collection such as making your semi-structured interview themes and associated questions more focussed.

A criticism that is always directed at case studies – and is even implicit in some of the ways in which some advocates of orthodox case studies suggest their use - is the extent to which their findings may be generalized. Clearly, the low numbers of case studies researched and the inability to employ the statistical logic that allows an author to make probabilistic inferences of occurrences that may be expressed as a scientific 'law' means that if your ambition in conducting your management inquiry is to generate only propositional statements that have wider applicability, case studies may not be the right choice. That is not to suggest that case studies cannot be used as a strategy of research that infers broader applicability and you may wish to use some of the strategies for generalization identified in Chapter 2 above. However, in academic research, generalization should not be privileged as a universal objective and as noted above, if the objective is to develop a deep, holistic understanding of a particular phenomenon that will resonate with those involved in the case and to provide and extend explanations of why things occur, case studies have distinct advantages. We would, thus, encourage you to be confident in expressing how you have realized the benefits of case studies explained above when writing up your research, rather than simply apologizing for case studies' limitations.

Case studies are often presented as being biased. In positivistic forms of orthodox case studies, bias is also seen as a problem. For example, Yin (2014: 20) says: 'The problems [of bias] are not different, but in case study research, they may occur more frequently and demand greater attention.' One source of bias may be seen to be a product of the orthodox approach. To achieve the different dimensions of validity discussed in Chapter 2, there is a need to derive from the literature in advance, what type of evidence is to be collected and from where. However, as noted, it is often not possible in practice to do exactly what was theorized in the research design to answer the research questions. Compromises may be made around the case to be studied, the participants whom you interview and the types of evidence that you collect. Unavoidable decisions about changing the details of your research design will introduce bias in this approach and the way to deal with this is by noting in your research diary why you changed what you did from your original research design and why the data that you have collected is a good surrogate for that which you intended to collect when you started your research. By keeping systematic records, you can provide an accurate account of your research in your dissertation and the reader will be able to understand its value.

Another reason why it is sometimes argued that bias appears in case studies is because there is often only one investigator, it is thought that the viewpoint will inevitably be biased. There are, however, limits to the merits of such a claim. The viewpoint that is expressed will be about evidence. One would expect that the data that has been collected, although biased in the sense of being directed towards the questions that the researcher wants answering, captures some essence of what the research participant wants to convey and so provides some information of value. Moreover, it is questionable whether bias is not an omnipresent element of any research project. It may be argued that those who strive to eliminate it are simply introducing a new bias of scientific discourse into their study under the name of objectivity. Furthermore, the passion that gives rise to bias can be helpful in defining the contents of a research project, sharpening focus and helping the researcher to keep going when an investigation becomes difficult. Thus, rather than seeking to eradicate all forms of bias, it is important to reflect on one's prospective biases and report them in the methodology chapter of your dissertation. Others can then decide the value of the work and the merits of the conclusions that you report and whether you have been sufficiently sensitive to your own biases to prevent them from influencing your report of your research in ways that devalue that work.

Another criticism that is often made of case studies is that they are often too long, disorganized and poorly informed by theory. It is indeed a challenge to organize disparate forms of data into a coherent story that not only reports on different forms of empirical evidence but also addresses others' published work so that it adds to theory. An important step in reducing the amount of information that is included and organizing it to tell the story of the case while addressing the theories of others is the stage of analysis. The different forms of analysis available to organize and interpret qualitative data are explained in other books in this series (see, for example, King and Brookes, 2017) and we have deliberately avoided a detailed discussion of analysis in this book. However, it is important to state that when analysing your case study evidence – regardless of the method of analysis that you choose – you should consider using the theories of others that relate to the focus in your case and organize your own data under the components of those theories to see the extent to which your findings support or suggest a different understanding to others. Data which does not fit under the headings that you choose can then be analysed to see whether it explains why your findings are different. Data which does not add to understanding may be ignored at that stage although it is important not to ignore data simply because it is *counter* to the argument that you are putting forward. If you have counter evidence, you should use that information to develop your argument further by, for example, stating the conditions under which your argument does not apply and providing the counter evidence. Following such a process would enable elimination of some data so that the case does not become too long and help to structure the discussion and incorporate others' ideas so that the case is informed by theory.

A final potential drawback of case studies relates to issues of ethics. These will be divided into two; those that relate to ethical procedures of universities and those that are a product of the research. The former arise because many universities nowadays expect researchers to report exactly what they are going to do in their research, even to the extent of asking for final drafts of research instruments such as questionnaires and interview schedules. This is often not possible, particularly with emergent case studies. As the time allowed for the conduct of the research with Masters dissertations is extremely limited, we would recommend that you use any existing knowledge of the case to indicate what you are most likely to do in the course of your research on your ethics application and find out what procedures you have to follow at your institution should your research take you beyond that. A common ethical problem that arises in the course of the research is – because of the small numbers in case study research – it sometimes becomes possible for the reader to identify the organization and even the individual participants from descriptions and job titles. Your supervisor may be able to advise you from drafts on whether your report of your research is in danger of doing this and needs changing. However, one way of avoiding doing this is by changing some of the details of the case that are not relevant to the substantive content of your investigation in ways that will help to disguise the case. For example, it may be possible to report that the organization is of a different size, or in a different location or sector, as long as these are not relevant to the argument that you are making. You should, however, report in the methodology chapter of your dissertation that you have changed some minor details about the organization to realize the desired level of anonymity.

CONCLUDING COMMENT

This book has been addressed to students whom we anticipate will need to complete a dissertation in a very short time period. Thus, although we have introduced such ideas about ways in which cases may be generalized and different units of analysis, our anticipation is that both the number of cases that will be conducted and the time taken to conduct the case will be limited. For this reason, we have deliberately avoided considering research strategies involving cases that require more resources – such as 'Before and after cases' where the researcher investigates the impact of a change, or 'Comparative case studies' where the researcher studies and theorizes the reasons for differences at comparable cases, although Mark's published study that is discussed in Chapter 5 gives some flavour of the latter. We hope, however, that success in a Masters dissertation involving the use of a case study will inspire the reader to consider using cases either for subsequent academic study or for researching professional challenges.

GLOSSARY

Abductive reasoning Combining inductive and deductive reasoning approaches (moving back and forth between theory and data) to choose or develop the most suitable theory for the pattern of evidence.

Access (1) The process of gaining entry (to a case study site) to undertake research. (2) The situation where a participant is willing to share data with the researcher. *See also*: cognitive access, physical access.

Analytic generalization Development of propositional knowledge that can be generalized, albeit not statistically, to other similar situations.

Bias A product of actions that deviate from the theoretical design in the course of the implementation of orthodox case studies.

Case A single instance, institution or phenomenon. *See also*: case study.

Case selection Rationale or method by which a researcher comes to study a particular case. *See:* census case selection, confirming or disconfirming case selection, criterion case selection, critical case selection, deviant case selection, extreme case selection, heterogeneous case selection, homogenous case selection, intensity case selection, maximum variety case selection, politically important case selection, purposeful random case selection, snowball case selection, stratified purposeful case selection, theory based case selection.

Case study protocol Guide for the collection of case study data comprising an overview of the research, the data collection procedures, actual questions that will be used to collect the data and a guide regarding how the research will be reported.

Case study Research strategy or strategic choice that seeks to develop a multi-dimensional understanding of one or a small number of instances, institutions or phenomena within its real-life context using a range of sources of evidence. *See also*: orthodox case study approach, emergent case study approach.

Census case selection Picking all cases in the entire population.

Chain case selection *See* snowball case selection.

Cognitive access Gaining agreement and access to collect data from individual participants.

Complete participant observation Data collection technique comprising participant observation in which the researcher participates fully in the activities being undertaken in the research setting.

Conceptualization level of explanation Articulation of a phenomenon's intrinsic qualities through defining the different ways in which it is distinct.

Confirming or disconfirming case selection Picking cases to either confirm or disconfirm a proposition.

Constructivist ontology Assumption that reality is complex and rich, being socially constructed through interaction between those participating.

Context bound level of explanation Linking of social, organizational or individual phenomena to their settings thereby drawing a range of differentiations and concepts into a broader schema.

Context free level of explanation Use of a meta-narrative that is applicable to a wide range of different situations.

Criterion case selection Using criteria identified in advance to pick cases that distinguish cases from others that make up the majority of a population.

Critical case selection Picking cases where theoretical propositions lead to the assumption that a phenomenon will either be present or absent.

Critical (literature) review Detailed and clearly justified commentary, analysis and summary of the literature pertinent to the research topic.

Deductive reasoning Testing theoretical propositions by collecting data for that purpose (moving from theory to data).

Deviant case selection   *See* extreme case selection.

Diary   *See* research diary, diary study.

Diary study   Data collection technique in which participants are asked to keep a (participant) diary recording events and/or experiences.

Differentiation level of explanation   Marking off or distinguishing of a metaphor from others, often by comparison or contrasting.

Embedded multiple cases   Two or more case studies, each comprising two or more sub units, all of which are analysed separately.

Embedded single case   One case study comprising two or more sub units that are analysed separately.

Emergent (case study) approach   Approach that views a case study as a strategic choice based on experiential, empathetic or tacit knowledge, in which the choice on how to conduct the research and its execution is made and evolves during the course of the research.

Emic knowledge   Knowledge derived from within (the case); often experiential, empathetic and tacit.

Empirical generalization   Development of propositional knowledge that can be generalized to a population on the basis of an empirical regularity or a pattern being observed.

Epistemology   Branch of philosophy concerned with assumptions about what constitutes acceptable, valid and legitimate knowledge. *See also*: interpretivist epistemology, positivist epistemology.

Etic knowledge   Knowledge that originates from outside (the case); often propositional.

Extreme case selection   Picking cases because they are unusual or extreme.

Focus group interview   Data collection technique comprising a group interview in which the topic is defined clearly and there is a focus on enabling discussion between the participants.

Gantt chart   Chart plotting the tasks or activities of a research project against a time line.

Gatekeeper   Person in the organization who controls access to that organization.

Generalization Development of propositional knowledge by inference from observing a particular manifestation of a phenomenon or system. *See also*: naturalistic generalization, analytic generalization, theoretical generalization, empirical generalization, small population generalization.

Grand level of explanation *See* context free level of explanation.

Group interview General term to describe the data collection technique comprising an interview conducted with two or more people.

Heterogeneous case selection *See* maximum variety case selection.

Holistic single case One case study analysed as a whole unit.

Homogenous case selection Picking a small sub-group from a wider population, which have definite shared characteristics or identity.

Inductive reasoning Using data already collected to develop theoretical propositions (moving from data to theory).

Informed consent Position achieved when participants are fully informed of the nature, purpose and use of the research and their role within it and agree to take part.

Institutional level (of understanding) Explanation focussing on understanding either an organization or sector (institution) within which the phenomenon of interest is manifest.

Intensity case selection Picking information rich cases that exhibit a lot of the qualities of the phenomena that are under consideration.

Interpretivist epistemology Assumption that theories and concepts are too simplistic and a focus on narratives, stories and perceptions recognizing there may be different interpretations and understandings of the same phenomenon.

Key informant Research participant who knows a considerable amount about the uniqueness and complexity of a case.

Level of understanding *See* institutional level of understanding, phenomenon level of understanding.

Levels of explanation *See* metaphor level of explanation, differentiation level of explanation, conceptualization level of explanation, context bound level of explanation, context free level of explanation.

Linear (case study) approach   *See* orthodox (case study) approach.

Maximum variety case selection   Picking cases to, between them, exhibit the variety of different characteristics that are found in the population as a whole.

Metaphor level of explanation   Use of a familiar form of experience or knowledge to make sense of something unfamiliar.

Multiple cases   Two or more case studies that are each analysed as a whole unit.

Naturalistic generalization   Development of propositional knowledge as a product of experience, being derived from tacit knowledge.

Observation   *See* participant observation, complete participant observation, structured participant observation.

Ontology   Branch of philosophy concerned with assumptions about the nature of reality or being. *See also*: constructivist ontology, realist ontology.

Opportunistic case selection   Picking cases on a basis of (1) on-the-spot decisions about their fit with the important criteria for the research, or (2) new criteria that become apparent in the course of the research, or (3) unforeseen opportunities of access that enable the problem under consideration to be addressed.

Orthodox (case study) approach   Approach that views a case study as a strategic choice based on propositional knowledge and having a clear protocol, in which the plan to conduct the research and the execution of the plan are primarily linear.

Participant diary   Written, audio or video diary, which a participant is asked to keep, recording events and/or experiences.

Participant observation   General term to describe data collection techniques comprising observation and recording of participants' behaviour in the research setting. *See also*: complete participant observation, structured participant observation.

Particularization   An approach that seeks to develop a deep understanding and explanations that capture the complexity of an individual case.

Phenomenon level (of understanding)   Explanation focussing on understanding a particular phenomenon or concept, rather than an institution.

Physical access   Gaining initial access to an organization to conduct research.

Pilot   Test of the method prior to the main data collection to minimize problems.

Politically important case selection   Picking cases that are politically sensitive as they allow illumination of particular types of problems that are also considered to be manifest elsewhere, but have come to light in a particularly damaging way in the politically important case.

Positivist epistemology   Assumption that knowledge comprises observable measurable facts that can be used to develop law-like generalizations and contribute causal explanations and predictions.

Primary data   Evidence collected specifically for the research project currently being undertaken.

Protocol   *See* case study protocol.

Purposeful random case selection   Picking cases using some form of random statistical method that offers all relevant cases equal chance of inclusion.

Questionnaire   General term comprising data collection techniques in which every respondent is asked to respond to the same set of questions in a predetermined order.

Realist ontology   Assumption that the realities of external phenomena are independent of individuals participating in them.

Reliability   Extent that a data collection method yields consistent data.

Research diary   Diary in which the researcher records chronologically aspects of the research project such as useful articles, potential data sources, discussions with their supervisor and thoughts about all aspects of the research.

Sample selection   The idea of a sample infers that the unit of analysis is part of a broader population. Although sample is a term that it is most appropriate to use when statistical methods are used to determine which units of analysis to study, some people also employ the term when studying cases that are not necessarily derived from a broader population. *See also*: Case selection.

Secondary data   Data originally collected for some other purpose than the research project currently being undertaken.

Selection of cases   *See* census case selection, confirming or disconfirming case selection, criterion case selection, critical case selection, deviant case selection, extreme case selection, heterogeneous case selection, homogenous case selection, intensity case selection, maximum variety case selection, politically important case selection, purposeful random case selection, snowball case selection, stratified purposeful case selection, theory-based case selection.

Semi-structured interview   Data collection technique using an interview where the research commences with a set of themes but is prepared to vary the order in which the questions are asked and include new questions if considered necessary.

Small population generalization   Development of propositional knowledge that can be generalized to a small population on the basis of the majority of cases having been studied.

Snowball case selection   Using people who are knowledgeable of the area or participants to suggest other cases that fit the selection criteria.

Stratified purposeful case selection   Picking systematically distinct clusters of cases within a population.

Structured participant observation   Data collection technique involving the observation and recording of participants' behaviour in the research setting using a high level of predetermined structure.

Theoretical generalization   *See* analytic generalization.

Theory   Systematic body of knowledge, grounded in evidence that can be used for explanatory or predictive purposes.

Theory-based selection   Picking cases on the bases of the recognition of evidence of important theoretical constructs at one or more cases.

Unstructured interview   Data collection technique using an interview which is loosely structured or informal without a fully formed predetermined list of themes to work through.

Validity   Criterion that is assumed to express the: (1) Extent that a data collection method measures what it is intended to measure. (2) Extent that research findings are about what they are stated to be about.

REFERENCES

Alvesson, M. and Sandberg, J. (2011) 'Generating research questions through problematisation', *Academy of Management Review*, 36(2): 247-271.

Bell, E. and Bryman, A. (2007) 'The ethics of management research: An exploratory content analysis', *British Journal of Management*, 18(1): 63-77.

Beynon, H. (1973) *Working for Ford*. London: Allen Lane.

Boblin, S.L., Ireland, S., Kirkpatrick, H. and Robertson, K. (2013) 'Using Stake's qualitative case study approach to explore implementation of evidence-based practice', *Qualitative Health Research*, 23(9): 1267-1275.

Bryman, A. and Bell, E. (2015) *Business Research Methods* (4th edition). Oxford: Oxford University Press.

Buchanan, D.A. (2012) 'Case studies in organizational research' in G. Symon and C. Cassell (eds), *Qualitative Organizational Research: Core Methods and Current Challenges*. London: Sage. pp. 351-370.

Buchanan, D., Boddy, D. and McCalman, J. (2013) 'Getting in, getting on, getting out and getting back', in A. Bryman (ed.), *Doing Research in Organisations*. London: Routledge Library Edition. pp. 53-67.

Burawoy, M. (1979) *Manufacturing Consent*. Chicago: Chicago University Press.

Campbell, D.T. (1984) 'Foreword' in R.K. Yin, *Case Study Research Design and* Methods. Los Angeles, CA: Sage.

Cassell, C. (2015) *Conducting Research Interviews*. London: Sage.

Clarkson, G.P. (2008) 'Diaries' in R. Thorpe and R. Holt (eds), *The Sage Dictionary of Qualitative Management Research*. Los Angeles, CA: Sage. pp. 79-80.

Collins, H.M. and Pinch, T.J. (1982) *Frames of Meaning: The Social Construction of Extraordinary Science*. London: Routledge & Kegan Paul.

Creswell, J. (2007) *Qualitative Inquiry and Research Design: Choosing Among Five Approaches*, 2nd edn. Thousand Oaks, CA: Sage.

Crowe, S., Cresswell, K., Robertson, A., Huby, G., Avery, A. and Sheikh, A. (2011) 'The case study approach' in *BMC Medical Research* Methodology. Available at:

http://bmcmedresmethodol.biomedcentral.com/articles/10.1186/1471-2288-11-100 (accessed 27 August 2016).

Department for Business Innovation and Skills (BIS) (2012) *SME Access to External Finance*, BIS Economics Paper Number 16. London: Department for Business Innovation and Skills.

Department for Business Innovation and Skills (BIS) (2013) *Evaluating Bank Lending to UK SMEs over 2001–2012: Ongoing Tight Credit?* London: Department for Business Innovation and Skills. Available at: www.gov.uk/government/uploads/system/uploads/attachment_data/file/193945/bis-13-857-evaluating-changes-in-bank-lending-to-uk-smes-2001-12.pdf (accessed 30 July 2016).

Department for Business Innovation and Skills (BIS) (2015) *Business Population Estimates for the UK and Regions 2015*. Available at: www.gov.uk/government/statistics/business-population-estimates-2015 (accessed 30 July 2016).

E&SSC (2002) *Select Committee on Education and Skills*, 3rd report. Available at: www.publications.parliament.uk/pa/cm200102/cmselect/cmeduski/561/ 56103.htm (accessed 15 June 2009).

Farquhar, J.D. (2012) *Case Study Research for Business*. London: Sage.

Foucault, M. (1980) *Power/knowledge: selected interviews and other writings, 1972-1977*. Brighton: Harvester Press.

Grant, R. (1996) 'Prospering in dynamically-competitive environments: Organizational capability as knowledge integration', *Organization Science*, 7: 375–387.

Gray, D.E., Saunders, M.N.K., Bristow, A. and Goregaokar, H. (2014) *Success in Challenging Times: Generating Social Capital*. London: Kingston Smith. Available at: epubs.surrey.ac.uk/805539/ [Accessed 10 May 2017].

Gray, D.E., Saunders, M.N.K. and Goregaokar, H. (2012) *Success in Challenging Times: Key Lessons for UK SMEs*. London: Kingston Smith LLP.

Gray, D.E., Saunders M.N.K. and Goregaokar, H. (2013) *SME Success in Challenging Times: Bank Finance – Lost in Translation*. London: Kingston Smith LLP. Available at: www.kingstonsmith.co.uk/media-and-resources/smes-and-bank-finance/ (accessed 12 October 2015).

Guo, S., Lumineau, F. and Lewicki, R.J. (2017) 'Revisiting the foundations of organizational distrust', *Foundations and Trends in Strategic Management*, 1(1): 1–88.

Hadjikakou, M., Chenoweth, J. and Miller, G. (2013) 'Estimating the direct and indirect water use of tourism in the Eastern Mediterranean', *Journal of Environmental Management*, 114: 548–556.

Halley, A., Nollet, J., Beaulieu, M., Roy, J. and Bigras, Y. (2010) 'The impact of the supply chain on core competencies and knowledge management: Directions for future research', *International Journal of Technology Management*, 49: 297–313.

Hansen, J.R. and Jacobsen, C.B. (2016) 'Changing strategy processes and strategy content in public sector organisations?', *British Journal of Management*, 27(2): 373–389.

Harris, L., Rae, A. and Misner, I (2012) 'Punching above their weight: The changing role of networking in SMEs', *Journal of Small Business and Enterprise Development*, 19(2): 335-351.

Hart, C. (1998) *Doing a Literature Review: Releasing the Social Science Research Imagination*. London: Sage.

Hartley, J. (2004) 'Case study research', in C. Cassell and G. Symon (eds), *Essential Guide to Qualitative Methods in Organizational Research*. London: Sage. pp. 323-333.

HM Treasury (2015) *2010 to 2015 Government Policy: Financial Services Regulation*. Available at: www.gov.uk/government/publications/2010-to-2015-government-policy-financial-services-regulation (accessed 30 September 2015).

Hookway, N (2008) 'Entering the blogosphere: Some strategies for using blogs in social research', *Qualitative Research*, 8(1): 91-113.

Jankowicz, A.D. (2005) *Business Research Projects* (4th edition). London: Thomson.

Johnson, P., Buehring, A., Cassell, C. and Symon, G. (2006) 'Evaluating qualitative management research: Towards a contingent criteriology', *International Journal of Management Reviews*, 8(3): 131-156.

Kahn, R. and Cannell, C. (1957) *The Dynamics of Interviewing*. New York: John Wiley.

King, N. and Brooks, J.M. (2017) *Template Analysis for Business and Management Students*. London: Sage.

Kogut, B. and Zander, U. (1992) 'Knowledge of the firm, combinative capabilities, and the replication of technology', *Organization Science*, 3: 383-397.

Krueger, R.A. and Casey, M.A. (2014) *Focus Groups: A Practical Guide for Applied Research*. London: Sage.

Kunisch, S., Menz, M. and Ambos, B. (2015) 'Changes at Corporate Headquarters: Review, integration and future research', *International Journal of Management Reviews*, 17: 356-381.

Lee, B., Collier, P.M. and Cullen, J. (2007) 'Reflections on the use of case studies in the accounting, management and organizational disciplines', *Qualitative Research in Organizations and Management: An International Journal*, 2(3): 169-178.

Lee, B. (2010) 'The individual learning account experiment in the UK: A conjunctural crisis?', *Critical Perspectives on Accounting*, 21(1): 18-30.

Lee, B. (2012) 'New public management, accounting, regulators and moral panics', *International Journal of Public Sector Management*, 25(3): 192-202.

Lee, T.W. (1999) *Using Qualitative Methods in Organizational Research*. London: Sage.

Lewicki, R.J., McAllister, D.J. and Bies, R.J. (1998) 'Trust and distrust: New relationships and realities', *Academy of Management Review*, 23(3): 438-458.

Lincoln, Y.S. and Guba, E.G. (1985) *Naturalistic Inquiry*. Newbury Park, CA: Sage.

Llewelyn, S. (2003) 'What counts as "theory" in qualitative management and accounting research? Introducing five levels of theorizing', *Accounting, Auditing & Accountability Journal*, 16 (4): 662-708.

Llewellyn, S. and Northcott, D. (2007) 'The "singular view" in management case studies', *Qualitative Research in Organizations and Management: An International Journal*, 2(3): 194-207.

Lupton, T. (1963) *On the Shop Floor*. London: Pergamon Press.

Marshall, C. and Rossman, G.B. (2011) *Designing Qualitative Research*, 5th edn. Thousand Oaks, CA: Sage.

Maslow, A.H. (1943) 'A theory of human motivation', *Psychological Review*, 50(4): 370.

Matheus, T., Saunders, M.N.K. and Chakraborty, S. (2016) 'Multiple dimensions of power influencing knowledge integration in supply chains', *R&D Management*, DOI: 10.1111/radm.12243.

McAreavey, R. and Muir, J. (2011) 'Research ethics committees: Values and power in higher education', *International Journal of Social Research Methodology*, 14(5): 391-405.

Mingers, J. (2000) 'What is it to be critical? Teaching a critical approach to management undergraduates', *Management Learning*, 31(2): 219-237.

National Audit Office (2002) *Individual Learning Accounts*, report by the comptroller and auditor general, HC1235 session 2001-2002, 25 October. London: The Stationery Office.

Nonaka, I. (1994) 'A dynamic theory of organizational knowledge creation', *Organization Science*, 5: 14-37.

Office for National Statistics (2015) *Business Demography 2015*. Available at: www.ons.gov.uk/ons/dcp171778_425087.pdf (accessed 6 April 2016).

Otley, D.T. and Berry, A.J. (1994) 'Case study research in management accounting and control', *Management Accounting Research*, 5(1): 45-65.

PAC (2003): *Individual Learning Accounts*, 10th report of session 2002-03, HC544. London: The Stationery Office.

Parlett, M. and Hamilton, D. (1976) 'Evaluation as illumination: A new approach to study of innovative programmes' in G. Glass (ed.), *Evaluation Studies Review Annual*, Vol 1. Beverley Hills, CA: Sage. pp. 140-157.

Patton, M.Q. (2015) *Qualitative Research & Evaluation Methods: Integrating Theory and Practice*, 4th edn. London: Sage.

Plakoyiannaki, E., Tzokas, N., Dimitratos, P. and Saren, M. (2008) 'How critical is employee orientation for customer relationship management? Insights from a case study', *Journal of Management Studies*, 45(2): 268-293.

Rebolledo, C. and Nollet, J. (2011) 'Learning from suppliers in the aerospace industry', *International Journal of Production Economics*, 129: 328-337.

Roy, D.F. (1959) '"Banana Time": Job satisfaction and informal interaction', *Human Organization*, 18(4): 158-168.

Saunders, M.N.K. (2012) 'Choosing research participants' in G. Symon and C. Cassell (eds), *The Practice of Qualitative Organizational Research: Core Methods and Current Challenges*. London: Sage. pp. 37–55.

Saunders, M.N.K. and Thornhill, A. (2004) 'Trust and mistrust in organizations: An exploration using an organizational justice framework', *European Journal of Work and Organizational Psychology*, 13(4): 493–515.

Saunders, M.N.K., Dietz, G. and Thornhill, A. (2014) 'Trust and distrust: Polar opposites, or independent but co-existing?', *Human Relations*, 67(6): 639–665.

Saunders, M., Lewis, P. and Thornhill, A. (2016) *Research Methods for Business Students*, 7th edn. Harlow: Pearson.

Schoonjans, B., Cauwenberge, P.V. and Bauwhede, H.V. (2013) 'Formal business networking and SME growth', *Small Business Economics*, 41: 169–181.

Sian, S. and Roberts, C. (2009) 'UK small owner-managed businesses: Accounting and financial reporting needs', *Journal of Small Business and Enterprise Development*, 16(2): 289–305.

Stake, R.E. (1995) *The Art of Case Study Research*. Thousand Oaks, CA: Sage.

Tashakkori, A. and Teddlie, C. (2010) *Sage Handbook of Mixed Methods in Social Research* (2nd edition). Thousand Oaks CA: Sage.

Taylor, F.W. (1911) *The Principles of Scientific Management*. New York: Harper & Brothers Publishers.

Thomas, G. (2016) *How to do Your Case Study: A Guide for Students and Researchers*, 2nd edn. London: Sage.

Tsang, E.W.K. (2014) 'Generalizing from research findings: The merits of case studies', *International Journal of Management Reviews*, 16(4): 369–383.

Vos, E., Jia-YuhYeh, A., Carter, S. and Tagg, S. (2007) 'The happy story of small business financing', *Journal of Banking and Finance*, 1(9): 2648–2672.

Wallace, M. and Wray, A. (2016) *Critical Reading and Writing for Postgraduates*, 3rd edn. London: Sage.

Yin, R.K. (2014) *Case Study Research Design and Methods*, 5th edn. Los Angeles, CA: Sage.

INDEX

Fold a Scorpion

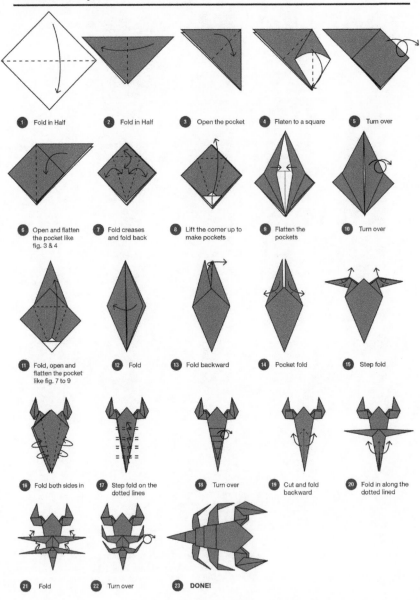

1. Fold in Half
2. Fold in Half
3. Open the pocket
4. Flaten to a square
5. Turn over
6. Open and flatten the pocket like fig. 3 & 4
7. Fold creases and fold back
8. Lift the corner up to make pockets
9. Flatten the pockets
10. Turn over
11. Fold, open and flatten the pocket like fig. 7 to 9
12. Fold
13. Fold backward
14. Pocket fold
15. Step fold
16. Fold both sides in
17. Step fold on the dotted lines
18. Turn over
19. Cut and fold backward
20. Fold in along the dotted lined
21. Fold
22. Turn over
23. DONE!